£3

HAD

HAD

The Tragedy of Crookham Court School

Ian Mucklejohn

KARNAC

First published in 2016 by
Karnac Books Ltd
118 Finchley Road
London NW3 5HT

British Library Cataloguing in Publication Data

A C.I.P. for this book is available from the British Library

ISBN-13: 978-1-78220-400-8

Typeset by V Publishing Solutions Pvt Ltd., Chennai, India

Printed in Great Britain by TJ International Ltd, Padstow, Cornwall

www.karnacbooks.com

This book is dedicated to all the children I have ever taught

We were all "had". All of us were duped. Only a few knew what was happening. Their victims were "had" in all senses of the word. But some of them have fought back and a few of the criminals, as yet just a few, have had what they deserve.

CONTENTS

AUTHOR'S NOTE

The use of real and false names in such a sensitive area has been based on certain criteria.

Real names are used:

- when a person has died;
- or has been successfully prosecuted;
- or when there has been a specific request for me to use a real name;
- but only when the victim's abuser has been successfully prosecuted;
- and/or if there is no link to a prosecution that may happen;
- and/or if the name/event is already in the public domain.

All other individuals are made unidentifiable.

A name is redacted if it may hinder a future prosecution.

In a single instance one person has become two.

Although names may have been changed, every event happened as described. Most pupils and adults were unaware of and unconnected with what was happening in secret.

ONE

Introduction

"When I'm grown up, daddy," said my seven-year-old son, Lars, "I want to be an English teacher at a prep school who does cross-country running in his free time." His English teacher at his prep school was a cross-country runner and, had he also been part of a knitting circle, no doubt Lars would have wanted to be in that, too. An inspirational teacher is one we do not forget.

Yet such is the hysteria that has gripped the nation following a few well-reported revelations—broadcast because they are unusual—that everyone in any situation connected with children is now considered potentially guilty until proven innocent.

"We take child protection extremely seriously" stated a bird sanctuary when they refused entry to a man unaccompanied by children. "Child protection" is a coverall term that assumes all children need protection from the paedophile that any adult might be. The very, very few have tarnished the reputation of the many; skewed our society to be mistrustful by default.

We all have had teachers in our lives. The vast majority are a superb influence on their pupils and appreciate the positive power they can exert on the young minds they nurture; kind, caring, educated, excellent communicators with the highest standards who want their pupils to gain from their interaction. They have an interest in children—an expression that can hardly be used now without being open to misinterpretation.

Abusive teachers, however, can continue for a long time. Their activities are so far removed from normal behaviour that their colleagues have no idea what they are doing. I know this from my own experiences.

I have met examples of the very, very few. They are attracted by certain circumstances. These came together in a mixture of naïveté, misjudgment, and dereliction at the school I taught at from 1969 which was, I thought at first, quirky, then ineffective, later malign, and ultimately criminal. From the start, I thought it was strange enough to write diaries about them while events were unfolding. These form a narrative showing the implosion of a school. From its darkest recesses, the sudden blaze of publicity at its denouement exposed secret crimes of sexual abuse that had been hidden for decades, so secret that only the perpetrators and victims knew of them.

Crookham Court became the most notorious school in the country.

The abusers were my colleagues; their victims were my pupils. I had no idea. After the closure of the school in 1989, the revelations continued. Several of my pupils contacted me, knowing that the way the school was run was never something I accepted, and knowing that they could trust me. I have always considered it an honour to be responsible for young people and a huge trust to be given charge of other people's children. I have run a summer course for decades and thousands have passed through my organisation having the time of their lives. For the young people in this book, this was a dark time. Researching it has been a humbling experience. Many have told me secrets that have been buried since childhood. All had different stories to tell; all have lives that have been defined by events that happened when they were in their early teens.

With only my experience as a human being to guide me, I look in this book at the institutionalised sexual abuse of boys, how it happened, how the signs could have been spotted, and how some have been helped to liberate themselves from the horrid feeling of complicity that has kept them from reporting the crimes committed against them. It shows how the climate of the times up to the closure of Crookham Court School in 1989 let these victims down; how head teachers, authorities, and even parents failed to report what they knew, fearful of the consequences, unaware of the wider implications, and certainly ignorant of the depth of the damage. On reading about the number of his abuser's other victims and the impact on their lives, one victim who had, against his initial judgment, decided to disclose to the police, told me of his amazement at how prolific his abuser was and how many lives he had touched. This is a pervasive and corrosive crime.

Crookham Court is just one example of a wider issue. Institutionalised abuse flourishes in darkness and secrecy. A bright light shone into the dark corners the abusers inhabit helps the boys they mistreated see themselves as victims; their abusers as criminals; the act as a crime to be reported. The victim's physiological reaction needs to be seen as simply that. There is no enjoyment, no complicity. Just reaction.

One of the criminals said, "Why can't they get over it?" This book explores the answer to this question in the frank and uncensored words of his victims.

I am privileged to have been taken into the confidence of many survivors of abuse. Some have disclosed to me, a person they have known, secrets hidden from their professional counsellors. They have given me an insight into this crime that they have denied others. This I share. Some have wished that their real names be used. Such are the long-term effects of abuse that I have, in almost every case, made the participants in this tragedy unidentifiable.

This book separates the minority of self-serving, perverted men who use the guise of teaching to prey on children from the vast majority of decent and dedicated professionals. It looks at how trust can be misplaced and how, by insisting on openness in everyday dealings, professionals can ensure that abuse can more easily be detected.

The tragedy of the institution that was created in 1961 and destroyed in 1989 is a lesson we can all learn from.

TWO

Parents, children, and the one who ended it all

The decades had rolled by. Peter, who had been a tousled fair-haired thirteen year old when I taught him, was a still good-looking man in his early forties whose set expression and lined brow spoke of issues that remained unresolved even at this distance in time. It was his testimony that had brought the edifice of his boarding school in West Berkshire crashing down; fixed its name into the national conscience through the headlines in every newspaper and TV screen; sent to prison several of those who had taught him.

But it was the lie that troubled him, that robbed him of his sleep, that made him feel guilty every time he washed and dressed one of his baby sons, that gnawed away at his confidence and left him as prone to the intimidation of others as he had been when a child.

"Peter doesn't want anyone to contact him. No one from his past. No one from the school," had been the reaction of his parents after the trial. I believed them, even though he had told me he wanted to externalise the events that had overwhelmed him. After many long years, I found that in fact it was his parents who could not confront what had happened to their son and not just to one of their sons, but to both of them. Both their sons had been sexually abused for years by different teachers at the school they had chosen to send their children to. Neither son had been aware that the other was being abused. The parents had seen the school, met the man who ran it and would abuse one of them and who would appoint to the staff the man who would abuse the other son. They were a "forces family" who had to travel at the behest of the British Army. In order to give their children the stability of one school in their lives, they were in receipt of a grant. This enabled them to send their sons to a boarding school, and how grand were the buildings and grounds they looked at. They met educators whose backgrounds were very different from their own; who had been to university; who had cut-glass accents; who inhabited a different world.

The world of the boys' boarding school that they had to make their choice from was largely a male dominated world. The men were charming, attentive, polite, cultivated. They, the customers, were charmed, attended to, beguiled, and seduced. The sons were carried along with this dream and were wafted from their council estate to the lofty pinnacles of the British public school, or so they thought. And they had every reason to assume this. The real public schools were out of the range of the armed forces grant, but by chance they happened upon a school whose fees were exactly the same as the money the government allowed them to spend.

They met the owner, a rather bumbling man, "a poppet" as another parent described him, and the headmaster, a man with bottle bottom glasses and a pleasant manner. They never asked if he were qualified. One doesn't do that. One makes assumptions. In fact, not that they had any reason to suspect, had they checked they would have found no university degree. And the rambling, ever so slightly eccentric owner, had they checked, had been dismissed from several schools and found that the only way he could keep a job down, a job that brought him into contact with boys, was to buy his own school. That was not a problem for him. His family had millions of pounds in its bank accounts. All he had to do was find a school to buy. Anyone with enough money can do this. There are plenty of teachers who need jobs and if you aren't too fussy about whom you pick, they will cover up your inadequacies. Every man has his price.

So this unassuming couple from a council estate on the south coast had their brief introduction to the cloistered world of the private school and, if they had looked at the fabric of the building and found, as the school inspectors had done, wiring coming away, stones cracking, "a dirty and depressing environment", would have seen it as it would have been presented to them—as part of the character of a huge building. And a school was a community, after all. More important than the physical surroundings was the atmosphere of camaraderie, the sound teaching, the bracing sports.

These unpretentious parents were happy to entrust their sons to the care of the people they had met, who had shaken them by the hand and looked them straight in the eye.

Within months each boy was naked, one in front of the owner, the other with the English teacher. Each was being masturbated and given oral sex. After they had left school, neither son had much desire to see his parents again.

How could they have known? How could anyone have suspected what horrors were happening behind the façade of this boarding school in West Berkshire? Through the words of the children, now adults, who came forward to tell me, their teacher, what had happened to them; who pushed aside the shame that their abusers had given them to ensure their continuing silence; who confronted those parts of themselves that still shamed them decades later; this is what I explore in this book.

And what signs were missed? What were the subtle hints that should have alerted right-minded people to the crimes that were being committed all around them? In fact, the signs were flashing, neon, screaming for attention. All were overlooked.

With one exception, one of the men who started the place, none of all the many sexual abusers at Crookham Court School would have shown up on any criminal records check, any disclosure and barring service. All of them were, in the eyes of the law, blameless. In fact, most had a string of offences behind them. Their victims had remained silent and, when a school had noticed, they had simply been moved on from school to school.

Peter and I sat in a smart restaurant in Winchester. His real name is not Peter, of course, but that has been the name given to him to protect his identity since 1989. So corrosive is sexual abuse that almost all the names in this book have been changed. It is the thoughts and actions that resound, not the details of the individuals. As a trusted teacher who has become a confidant to many, the secrets of their identity will stay with me. There have been some who have regretted their candour and I hope will not recognise themselves. One person has become two people, but all the events and conversations have happened. Much of this book was written contemporaneously as a record of a phenomenon before I knew what was really happening. No one knew. No one was to know. The secrets were hidden well.

For years Peter had been abused by the owner of Crookham Court School, Philip Cadman, but it was after he left and when he discovered that his brother, Barry, had been abused by the English teacher that he acted. He wrote a letter to ChildLine describing the abuse he had suffered. Its director, Hereward Harrison, took the letter to Esther Rantzen who was so stunned by the contents that she let it sit on her desk for some time before taking action. When she did, it was devastating. The case was investigated, children and staff were interviewed, and the scandal was exposed on Esther's prime-time *That's Life!* in June 1989 on three successive Sunday nights—a television programme that, at its peak, had an audience of 18 million. It made headline news. In the fullness of time, Cadman and two other teachers—one of whom was Barry's abuser—were arrested, tried, convicted, and jailed.

Peter had visited me several times in the interim. I knew—and he knew that I knew—that there was more. A quarter of a century after the court case in which he stood in front of a jury and described the abuse that had been inflicted on him, he still had not told the whole story (personal conversation, October 2008):

> "There's something else," he said. "I've never told anyone about it." He paused, looked at me and said, "And I'm not going to say anything now."
>
> "OK, Peter. That you're telling me you're not going to tell me tells me you are. Shall I prise it out of you with questioning, or will you just come out with it? You know I won't judge you. I never have. Whatever happened, you were a thirteen-year-old boy who should never have been placed in the situations you were placed in. You say you put yourself in those situations. Well, you didn't. You were put there by a person whose responsibility it was to protect you."

What was going to come out was not for the ears of the genteel Winchester public who surrounded us. We left the restaurant and drove to my home.

What he told me, he later wrote down (email, 12 November 2008):

> Once again I found myself standing at the threshold of his door. A big white door with the standard, blue, "Fire door. Please keep shut" sign. Unlocked as always, it was the dividing point between my life as a schoolboy and something altogether different.
>
> I both knew and did not know what lay beyond. To my left there would be a marble slab used as a radiator cover. Sitting on top of the slab, next to the sash window, was an object of great desire, a grey dial telephone. A telephone,

a contact with friends, the wide world, or even home. For boys with little money, many of who were from overseas, this particular phone was a challenge. It was a challenge to try and make calls from it without getting caught. The old Georgian sash window where the phone was situated stood no chance of resisting the knife, stolen from the cutlery tray in the dining room. Once opened, a couple of the pupils would climb outside onto the lobby roof and then, closing the window behind them, would walk along to the next window where the telephone was positioned. The second pupil would continue to walk to the next window and act as a lookout. The call having been made, the boys would then swap roles, one becoming the lookout and the other becoming the trespasser. I always thought that this was a strange place to put a telephone. It was never moved, not even when the bill came through with unexplained calls to numbers abroad.

Opposite the phone was his bathroom. This was filthy. It was blue and dark green. The blue was paint; the dark green was mould. The shower curtain, spotted black as it was drawn against the wall, crumpled in a clutter. The mirror spoke of years of water, shaving cream, and toothpaste. In the corner, behind the door, was his pile of dirty washing. I knew this because I had often gathered the clothes together against the wall and used it as a hiding place on more than a few occasions. The stench of his unwashed clothes reminded me of what I was hiding away from in the first place.

As I continued down the corridor, the curve of the hallway bore left. There was a door that was always on the latch; a door that led to the junior dormitories and another that was locked, a door that led to the senior dorms and staff accommodation. And there in front of me was another white door. This was the doorway that led to his bedroom. This was always kept locked. Whether it was from the outside or the inside, this door was always locked.

On the right was another door. The door. This was the door that led to his study. The door that led to many other things besides. I took a deep breath, knocked a couple of times, and anticipated an answer. There it was. I entered the room knowing full well what I needed to say.

As usual, the room was full of smoke. The smoke carried a distinctive smell of Drum tobacco and was being inhaled through one of his small collection of pipes. On this occasion, he was alone and was sitting at his desk doing his accounts.

He was always pleased to see me. We got the niceties out of the way first. He asked me how I was keeping and I returned the question. Just to spark up some "normal" conversation I asked him about his accounts and whether the school was making enough money for him to retire. He told me that the school was running at a loss. As I calculated how this was possible, I found myself drifting away from what I needed to say.

It had been four years since we had gone into Caddy's flat, my friends and me. It was something to do. He didn't mind. In fact, he welcomed us in there. Who knows? There might even be something to take, I thought. There were four of us. We mooched around, chatted, were cheeky, everything that might be expected from thirteen year olds. Caddy enjoyed it.

After a while the others left, bored. They wanted to do something else. Caddy went out with them. Oh yes, he'd enjoyed having them there. I'd seen it in his little piggy eyes, seen the smile, seen the interest. And I wondered, oh how I wondered. What sort of interest was this? No, more than that, I knew what it was. All of a sudden I felt a power that I had never felt before. I knew what this man was about. I knew that I could use this power for my benefit. I looked around the flat. Safe, drawers, cupboards, some locked; some not, but all there at arm's length for opening and for taking. Drawers stuffed full of papers. Chequebooks, coins, notes. The man was rich. Everyone said he was a millionaire. Must have been to have bought this place. And he was chaotic, everything was in a state. There was no order. Letters, papers, documents of all kinds lay piled by chairs, had drifted into corners. If there was an empty surface, some piece of paper would be on it. I moved some. He would never know. Whatever I did, he would never know. I could take. I could steal. It could be Christmas and birthday rolled into one. All I had to do was get in there. I knew where the answer lay.

It took me twenty-five years before I could tell anyone what I did. Everyone said I was the victim, but I knew that it had been me who started it, started the events that went on and on for four years. On and on and back and back I came. I was thirteen and I was guilty. No matter what anyone said through the years of counselling, this was what I had started, not only started, but continued, nurtured, fed, developed. I had the power. For the first time, I knew that I could shape the way my life was. What else was there? A humdrum home on a housing estate with parents who were just a mum and dad who accommodated me and with whom I had nothing special in common. We talked, but never about what mattered. By the time I was thirteen, not a word about sex had been mentioned. Until the day I left home, there was nothing said about this, or feelings, or growing up, or anything. These were people I lived with, nothing more. At school, it was different. There was where freedom lay. There were people who talked, laughed, had a magic about them and, oh, how I wanted this to carry on. But if I said, if I told, if ever one word leaked out, it would all stop.

I had the power all right. Big power, but only as long as I said nothing. That's all I had to do, just keep the secret. I couldn't tell. But that was just as well because it was all my fault. If I hadn't done what I did, nothing would have happened. I was the one responsible, but I was in control and this was what I had wanted. A generation later I took my courage in both hands and told my secret. I pulled out of the black recesses of my mind what I had lived with for all my adult life and gave it words, words that were prised out of me, but were, in the end, my own. These were blunt words which told of a basic act, a base act. It was the path I had chosen and never, in all those years of guilt, had I been able to see it any other way. That revelation took time and the patience of kind hearts.

How simple it had been for my thirteen-year-old self. I see him now in his school uniform, blue shirt, blue pullover, grey trousers. He looks at the trajectory from the front door of the flat to the sitting room. There, just around the corner. That's the best place. I see him walk there with the confidence that comes from knowing what he is doing. I see him unclasp the waistband, unzip the flies, let the trousers fall to the ankles. I see him sit in the upright chair against the wall just out of sight of the door. I see the legs open, the thin white cotton underpants covering the prize.

All I had to do was wait. I knew it was going to happen. I was pretty sure I knew how it would happen. There was the bait. I was the spider. That the web was his had not occurred to me and would not do so for many years.

I jolted my mind back into focus. I told him straight. It had to stop. There would be no more fiddling, no more getting me to put my hands down his trousers. The anxious moments had to stop. As well as the sexual moments. I hated the thought of being walked in on in an awkward position. What would people think of me?

Of course, we would remain friends (I was young at the time!). I would still come and talk to him as normal people would. Tea and biscuits would still happen but without the favours. To make this stop I had to tell him something convincing, something that would make him feel guilty about what he was doing. I told him I had a girlfriend. I had met her at one of the school discos. I told him that I didn't want to cheat on her so I told him the sexual stuff had to stop. I gave twenty other reasons why it had to stop, always giving a reason, never making a threat.

I was quite surprised when he unexpectedly said yes, it will stop. Just as suddenly as it had started, he told me it was going to end.

As I walked out of the flat, for the first time since it started I was feeling in control. Although I had always felt responsible for being in this situation, I had never felt in control. On this day, I did.

Now I know, of course, I was never in control at all. There was a reason for the door always being on the latch; the door that led to the junior dormitories and not the door that led to the senior or staff accommodation. And the telephone, this of course was the honeypot that attracted boys through the unlocked door. While we thought one of us was keeping an eye out for the other, he knew all along that there were boys in his flat.

Now I can see it. The accounts were right; the school was losing money. It was being run at a loss. The fees came in at below the allowance that was allocated for the families in the forces. These families lived abroad and all they wanted was for their children to be educated in England. The low fees were what attracted the families to the school. And in they came, the boys whose parents lived far away, who had no family in this country, who depended on the kindness of those who were in loco parentis.

> Of course, he had always been pleased to see me. Every time I was within his four walls, something happened. Of course he was going to tell me that it would stop and that it would never happen again. Oh yes, it would never happen again. He told me this on several occasions. And it never did—until the next time.
>
> As I left that room feeling confident this was the end, there was only one person in control that day and it wasn't me.

Peter remained wracked by the guilt of that single action. "They say no child ever asks for sex. But I did," he told me. His eyes were focused on the floor.

"He put you in that situation, Peter. He gave you enough clues for you to know what he wanted and what there was in it for you if you gave him it. You wrote that you weren't in control and you need to believe that you weren't. You did what he had cleverly put into your mind to do and what should an adult do when a child does something like that? Well, you know, and it certainly isn't what he did. Whatever you were imagining might happen was not what in your wildest dreams you might have supposed. You didn't make a move on him. He made a move on you."

Much as the two people he told tried, Peter's fundamental belief in his complicity was hard to shake and was insidious in its chipping away at his self-confidence as a man and as a father to two children. The events and what he saw as their causation had defined his life from the age of thirteen. He saw it and hated it and in hating it, hated himself.

But the truth sometimes takes a while to distil. What Peter wrote was not how it happened. Two more years were to elapse before he would reveal his entire secret (personal conversation, 18 February 2010).

"It wasn't quite like that was it? Tell me about the 'thin fabric'."

He looked me straight in the eye. The time was right. The trust was there. He knew I knew anyway and he knew he would not be betrayed by me. There was no fabric between Cadman and "the prize". Peter had dropped his underpants while Cadman was out. By the time he returned, Peter was exposed. "Yes, I was playing with myself," he said. Nearly thirty years after the event, he had finally told the truth. Yes, of course, Cadman should have told him to put it away and, yes of course, Cadman had cleverly got him in his flat alone with plenty of coded messages as to what he was interested in and what Peter had to gain. It was a seventy-year-old man, not a thirteen-year-old boy, who had put him in this position.

"He was always kind to me. He never hurt me." Peter really believed this. By this time, Peter was estranged from his mother, father, and brother. He found social interaction difficult and had been through several jobs. He had been to the High Court, had received hours of counselling and was, he admitted, finding his depression hard to cope with. Yet, he had never blamed Cadman; had never accepted that he had been abused, hurt just as effectively as if his childish innocence had been ripped from him. His perceived complicity, his adherence to Cadman's guiltlessness and his belief that he had been responsible for the closure of the school added other layers to the abuse and gave him even more guilt to overcome in adulthood.

The words "He should never have done this" have never been spoken by him.

Now it was all out. He had finally given voice to the secret, broken the taboo, had uttered the words that had been known to him alone and only at this point did he understand that he had really freed himself. Or, at least, loosened the chains.

On the Crookham Court Facebook page I created as an outlet for its pupils, Peter added a message in April 2013 saying that the school and building, friends and memories meant everything to him.

It was a place that had so damaged him, yet he could see it now as the springboard that had brought him into contact with famous people like Esther Rantzen and Princess Diana, that had let him meet the great and good at Esther's launch of *Running Out of Tears* at Speaker's House; that had given him a TV presence. It had been a point he had not moved on from. Until he had brought it all out, he had remained in the role of an abused child who didn't feel he had been abused, but had to accept that he had been as this was what the world was telling him.

On 11 September 2013, Peter again posted on Facebook to say that for many, 11 September is remembered for the awful things that happened in America and that, for him, it would always be remembered as the day he had started at Crookham Court thirty years before.

He wrote that it had changed his life, that he had met some nice people and had the best times of his younger life there and that while the bad times were slowly becoming a distant memory, the good times were as fresh as the day he started. He considered that Crookham would always mean a lot to him and with pages like the one he was writing on, his fond memories of all the better times would continue. He affirmed that Crookham meant so much to him and even today, he was still pleased to have attended it.

He knew that the school had betrayed him, just like it had betrayed his parents. I wondered how on earth they felt knowing they had put him there.

There was too much history for Peter to see anything from his parents' perspective. If there had been any perception of the need to forgive or of any understanding of the guilt that they might feel, it had long ago been subsumed by indifference.

(Personal conversation, 29 October 2010):

> We never talked about sex when I was young. We never talked about anything much. It was all just boring. I don't

think they cared. Crookham was much better than life on the estate. My mother just told me what to do. She carried on telling me what to do. I don't have much to do with them now.

My brother tells me not to be identified as that'll involve him. I haven't spoken to him for two years.

You know, even now people try to bully me and I can't stand up to them. That's what happens at work.

From the wreckage of his childhood, nothing was unscathed. Peter's wider family was in pieces. His parents had sent their children away to be looked after by others and whatever assumptions they might have made that they would be nurtured were torn apart. Had they been more sensitive, maybe they would have noticed the changes. They paid a heavy price for not picking up on what vibrations there might have been; for assuming that upper-class professional men had the highest moral standards; for putting their trust in a school.

"So now you have your own family and at least you know what not to do," I told Peter.

He hugged his son.

"But it would be nice for him know his grandparents."

THREE

Carelessness

"Care", "duty of care", and "in the care of" are terms much used to convey legal responsibilities. All children are in the "care" of a person or an organisation until they are grown up. That the care involves sheltering and protection is clear, yet there is also the concept of "being careful with" and "taking care" in its broadest terms, not only of those who are to be cared for, but being careful enough to look at the fundamentals of the structure that provides the care.

For various reasons, insufficient care was taken back in the days Crookham Court School was founded. "Lack of due diligence", it would be termed in the twenty-first century. The carelessness was not cavalier, but a bit of short-sightedness here was compounded by an oversight there until the foundation of the structure was undermined. It helps to look at the history of the concept and the man who had the original idea.

Lt. Commander Robert Smithwick was a tall, Edwardian-looking, former naval officer, upright in stance and clipped in verbal delivery. His moustached upper lip was stiff and he took what was to be taken on his bearded chin. He did reserve as only the British know how. His career in the Royal Navy was a distinguished one and he left it in 1960 with a lump sum and a pension. Many years later, when I came to know him as a warm-hearted and convivial man and felt able to use his first name and he mine, he told me he was fortunate to have the chance to embark on a second career. He decided to start a school. Pooling his payout with his wife Rosemary's money, he looked for a suitable location to do this. He visited several houses in 1960. One of these was Crookham House. Built for the Tull family in the middle of the nineteenth century and having had a variety of institutional uses ranging from the wartime headquarters of the Great Western Railway to a school for the families of the service personnel at the US Air Force base on Greenham Common opposite, it was known locally as "the Blind House" because of its boarded-up windows.

Robert wrote about its purchase in the *Crookham Court Chronicle*, the school magazine, in 1972:

> In the winter of 1960, a bleak, boarded-up, broken-into, battered Crookham House was visited; a tour of the house, as well as showing the innumerable leaks, signs of dry rot and general damage visible by torchlight did also demonstrate its possibilities as a school—the price, however, precluded further hope. That winter was spent in scanning advertisements, making forays to hopeful-sounding properties, all with the same lack of success. So, in the spring of 1961, with one boy already booked for the new school, still non-existent, a return to Crookham was made in desperation to see if the owner was now prepared to drop his price. The depredations of a winter's weather plus frequent visits of vandals to break into and damage the house, thefts of lead in roofing, drainpipies, etc. had impressed upon the owner the desirability, nay, the necessity of getting rid of it quickly, while there was some portion of the fabric remaining. A bargain reasonably satisfactory to both sides was, therefore, quickly concluded. On May 15th 1961, possession of Crookham House—renamed Crookham Court—was obtained.

> Daily, it seemed, more and more applications to see over the proposed school were received and in spite of many rooms having to be shown off by torchlight and interviews conducted in a carpet-less room on wooden chairs, it soon became clear that initial numbers would be nearer thirty than ten. As the days shortened and September advanced, activity in the house reached a crescendo and work frequently went on into the small hours. Well remembered are the thrill of the first coat of polish on the hall floor, the first time the ancient hot water system was lit and actually produced hot water from the taps, the first heat coming through the antiquated central heating system and numerous other "firsts". It was a motley crew that assembled at 4.00 p.m. on Friday 22nd September 1961 to give meaning to that newly painted and erected board in front of the house: "Crookham Court—Boarding School for Boys". After a gap of several years, life had returned to Crookham House.—Lt. Commander R. S. Smithwick.

Robert's enthusiasm is palpable in his writing. "One boy already booked." Into what? There was no school, no stated ethos, to book into. These parents' blind trust in something that did not even exist, something that could not be assessed on any rational basis meant that they were unwittingly, but quite happily, booking their child into a school that would be run by a convicted sex offender, the headmaster, Roy Cotton.

When it was created in 1961, Crookham Court was a public school in miniature. Chapel at the start of the day, lessons, games every afternoon, more lessons, prep, and the occasional outing. Apparently traditional, solid, reliable. The houses were named after local rivers: Kennet, Avon, Enborne. I wondered why there were just three when four would have been easier for team games. The truth was that such a small school—Robert had thought in terms of 100 or so boarders—did not need a house system. The building was nuclear and the dormitories were grouped by age. The concept of house arose only in terms of sport and the housemasters assumed some pastoral responsibility for their charges. By and large, though, everyone knew everyone else and the boys gravitated to whoever appeared most congenial. In a building that was essentially stripped of the comforts of home and in which the regime was strict and military, to take tea with a teacher, sit in a soft chair, and feel carpet under the feet was enough of a treat to ensure that master's popularity. Several masters knew that this was attraction enough to get a child inside.

The school was run on a shoestring. He told me he dreaded the moment when the heating failed as it would take all his profit to replace the boiler. The school he created was as much his baby as his two young children.

Robert Smithwick was a leader. He was focused, upright, and determined. "I only did it once," he admitted to me after the boys had burst out laughing at him one lunchtime. "Now those on shore leave this afternoon …" he had started. He got no further. "I knew it would happen sometime. I've done very well up to now."

As a leader, a commander (he retained his naval rank as a title), he was used to taking charge and doing things his way, used to giving orders, but he was not a teacher and without specific qualifications to be in charge of children, not that these were needed in 1961. There was also something else that he was not, a weakness that he revealed to me quite casually in conversation; a perfectly normal human weakness that is shared by many of us, but which in this case had ramifications that would endure. "Trouble is, I'm a really bad judge of character," he told me.

"A really bad judge of character." It was a throwaway remark, said almost light-heartedly, but it became the theme of the tragedy that unfolded. It's the word "judge" that strikes me. Robert started the school as a hobby; something to do.

Hobbies are pastimes, hobbies occupy one's free time and stop one getting bored. But Robert was a "judge". He was also "the jury". In the small world of a boarding school that he created, he was judge and jury. All the powers were his and he enjoyed an unwonted omnipotence. He never saw it as such and would not have wanted it. Nevertheless, his inability to judge assumed enormous proportions. Not being a good judge of character can cause you problems, but when you create a school, you assume a responsibility for all the lives in it and it's not just to you this can give problems. Robert Smithwick took on his shoulders the burden of this responsibility no doubt without wholly realising its implications. The conclusion may have come earlier, but ultimately it was the media that tested it and found that it was lacking. By the time he externalised into words his fatal flaw, the damage had been done. Each time he misjudged someone's character, lives were changed.

Was it his taking for granted that others shared his straightforwardness? Back then, teachers were assumed to have an exalted status over the common throng. They were professionals and there was an assumption that dedication to this profession precluded any base activity. It was an assumption that was to blind all of us to what was to happen later in the school's existence.

And that was then. All of us were more trusting, less jaundiced. Schools are for those who take an interest in children and boarding schools can do a superb job in creating a stimulating environment for youngsters to develop in. Most children love their schooldays and benefit hugely from them. Many children who were at Crookham Court had a great time, even when the school was imploding, frisking around like puppies with hardly anyone to control them. Several have told me that these were the best days of their life, even though terrible things were also happening to them. For many of them, their home lives were unutterably dull, communication with their parents was next-to-none, and school was a chance to be free from the constraints of tedium.

Robert Smithwick died before the allegations against Roy Cotton became widely known and, in the absence of other input, I have relied for background on evidence in the *Independent Historic Cases Review 2008/9*, commissioned by the Bishop of Chichester for the Church of England, published in redacted form in February 2012, produced by Roger Meekings. It provides a brief chronology of the man selected by Robert Smithwick to be in charge of young boys in the newly-formed Crookham Court School. The following table is directly from the report (date; event; comment (in italics)):

10 April 29	Born Ventnor, Isle of Wight.
(Undated)	Sandown Secondary Grammar School.
27 May 47	National Service leading writer [educational and vocational instruction]. Uncertified teacher St. Catherine's Home, Isle of Wight [a C of E home for children recovering from illness].
31 Dec 47	Cotton applies for the ministry.
14 Jan 48	Positive reference from St. Catherine's Home but described as immature.
11–14 July 49	Attended selection conference and was recommended for training. Attends Ripon Hall, Oxford [theological college].
2.2.51–12.2.54	Assistant scout master, Oxford.
Feb 54	Abingdon Magistrates Court. Convicted of indecent behaviour with a child. Sentenced to 1 year probation. *There is no third party information to confirm the charges and the nature of the conviction. No one from the college appears to have attended and recorded the outcome. One explanation for this is that Cotton might not have revealed details of his court appearance until after the event. Note that the letter from Scout HQ 24.10.68 refers*

	to the offence as indecent assault on a young boy and states that the record indicates that RC is "a person who may have no connection whatsoever with the Movement." This was about six weeks prior to ordination.
16 Mar 54	Letter from Bishop Allen, Principal of Ripon Hall Oxford to CATCM, Westminster: "Right up to the end Cotton maintained that he had done nothing of which he was ashamed … The magistrates found him guilty and gave the minimum sentence that he should be 'on probation' for one year. … I have said to him that it need not necessarily prejudice his ordination for all his life … He was in any case a rather weak, immature character." *In fact, this was not the "minimum" sentence available. Cotton could have received a conditional discharge or a fine. Probation would have been at their disposal if the magistrates felt the person required supervision/direction.*
1961	Appointed as a master in an independent school in Fareham before moving to a school in Newbury.
Summer 1961	Reader in Oxford Diocese. Believed to have gone into partnership with Commander Smithwick to start a new Prep school, at Crookham Court, Newbury.
3 May 66	Letter from Bishop of Portsmouth to Commander Smithwick, Crookham Court: "Roy Cotton and the Vicar of Thatcham came to see me yesterday and I heard the sad story of Roy's dismissal by you. … we did discuss the future and particularly in terms of Roy's ordination … . What I am concerned about is that possibly you have information which I ought

	to be aware of and I should be grateful if you could write to me about it. I have been aware all the way along of the incident 12 years ago when he was put on probation. As far as I am concerned I would want to write that past off, unless there were good reasons for not doing so." *No response from Commander Smithwick on the Blue File.*
May 66	Letter from Bishop of Portsmouth to Bishop of Norwich: "RC came to see me … about the possibility of ordination. On looking at the files I see there is a note with 'no step to be taken without reference to me' and I have no doubt this reference refers to his appearance in court in 1954 … . This is now 12 years ago and as far as I can make out there has been no hint of any further trouble since. I should be grateful if you could let me have a line, not least to clear the decks." *There is nothing on the current Blue File that refers to this. It does look as if there might have been a "hint" of further trouble [see 4 May 66].*
4 May 66	Note by GT [?] [for file with a copy to the bishop] on Roy Cotton: "He came to see me on May 4th at the bishop's suggestion. I found him in a state of considerable distress and tension … . His partner in the school in which he works, Commander Smithwick, has given him notice to leave in July or December, as a result of allegations made or insinuated by boys at the school … . Found him a strange personality, and although it may very well be that the allegations are untrue and unfounded, I think I can sense a little of the atmosphere which caused them to be made. If the bishop is satisfied

he could be ordained, and I understand that Commander Smithwick is prepared to back him, should some reference be made back to the Bishop of Derby who was principal of his theological college when the first incident occurred which Roy says never took place … ."
Issue of "allegations made or insinuated by boys at the school". No record on file that these were identified or investigated. Cotton appears to be denying, on this occasion, that the 1954 incident happened.

5 May 66 — Letter from Bishop of Norwich to Bishop of Portsmouth: "I would have thought that if there has been no hint of any further trouble it would be quite in order to consider Roy Cotton for ordination … ."

13 May 66 — Letter from Bishop of Portsmouth to Archbishop of Canterbury outlining RC history [including criminal offence] and his repeated requests to be considered for ordination: "… at the time he protested his innocence, and he has done ever since, and in fact from that time has been teaching … he has been to see me on three occasions. I have seen his partner in the school, the Bishop of Derby, and saw his principal who was in office, when the alleged offence occurred; the Bishop of Norwich who was concerned with him as an ordinand. And all are agreed that as there has been no indication of any further trouble for the last twelve years, it would be right for him to be considered … I am not sure whether having been convicted there would need to be a dispensation from you and I would be most grateful for your guidance in this matter … Cotton is a man of considerable ability … and I cannot think that having been

so free of any trouble for twelve years that there is a likelihood of there being any problem in the future." *The principal of the theological college had become the Bishop of Derby. RC managed to collect a good deal of sympathy from a number of senior clerical sources. Bishop of Portsmouth even goes so far as to put his case to the archbishop. He also describes RC as a "man of considerable ability". This is far from the picture that was apparent even at that time by reference to what is recorded on the file; there were doubts about his "character". The offence in 1954 appears to be "downgraded" or reconstructed as "the alleged offence" and there is emphasis placed on RC's persistent denial that he did anything wrong.*

17 May 66 — Response from archbishop [secretary]: The archbishop "is reassured by what you have said and thinks you would do right to consider ordaining him to a title in the carefully selected parish which you mention".

2 June 66 — Letter from principal, theological college, Chichester to Bishop of Portsmouth regarding a meeting with RC. He goes on to say: "… we are happy to take him here for two terms, with a view to ordination at Advent, assuming you are taking responsibility for sponsoring him and that you have cleared his past and that you will square things with the ACCM … . I hope to see him [the Bishop of Derby] in Cuddesdon … and I want to find out why he did not stand up for Cotton in 1953 [something which rather rankled with Cotton]." *There is no evidence that the matter was "squared" with ACCM.*

2 June 66 — Letter from +Portsmouth to Advisory Council for the Church's Ministry, ACCM, expressing

the hope that the normal rules can be stretched regarding RC. Past history is explained as is his partnership with Commander Smithwick in a school in Newbury: "Now, alas, news of his previous conviction has caught up and Cmr Smithwick, his partner, has felt obliged to tell him that they must part company. I have had a long talk with Cmr Smithwick and with the Vicar of Thatcham, whom Cotton has been assisting as a reader, I have talked to +Derby, who was his principal at Rippon Hall and I have seen those who have passed on gossip from this locality, and find no truth whatsoever in the allegations which have been made. I referred it to the archbishop and ... he thinks I should do right to ordain him ... to a carefully selected parish. ... and what I am asking is that he [Cotton] might be excused from coming to a further selection conference and be allowed to complete a quiet two to three terms before ordination. My reason for making this request is on pastoral grounds. He has been pretty desperately hurt by the turn of events and I believe it could be wrong for him to have to go over and over the whole story again. I can find no evidence of homosexual tendencies, indeed he has been engaged once and has a prospective girlfriend at the moment. Over these last twelve years he has been taking boys away to the Continent and there has been no breath of suspicion. But I do think it would be really harmful to him if he had to go over the whole business again in a group at a selection conference. I hope, therefore, there may be some way in which I may be whitewashed if I simply go

	ahead." *What the gossip was about Cotton is not explained. Was it the allegations or insinuations from the boys at the school [cf. GT above, 4 May]. Or was it, as +Portsmouth puts it, news of his previous conviction catching up. It may be more likely to be the former given that +Portsmouth saw "those who passed on the gossip locally" and decided the allegations had no truth.*
8 June 66	Letter from ACCM to Bishop of Portsmouth refers to Bishop of Portsmouth's letter of 2 June. ACCM suggests that it should go to the selection committee, with an assessment from Dr. Backus, psychiatric adviser. *Portsmouth letter of 2 June not on file.*
15 June 66	Response from +Portsmouth to ACCM: accepting the proposal that RC sees Dr. Backus but not accepting need for RC to go to selection committee and says he will discuss with +Ely.
17 June 66	Letter from +Portsmouth to ACCM: "I have now been able to talk things over with +Ely. The latter was quite clear that Cotton ought not to be required to meet any members of the selection committee; and felt too that unless Cotton himself expressly wished it, he should not be required to see Dr. Backus. I am, therefore, sending Cotton to Chichester for two terms, with the proviso that the situation will be reviewed at the end of his first term, and if all goes well I will ordain him at Advent … ."
20 June 66	Letter from ACCM to +Portsmouth, accepting the position but suggesting a medical for RC "so that he does not feel that he is an exception in every respect". *A pleasant enough letter from ACCM but with a heavy barb at the end, which emphasises the unusualness of the situation.*

20 June 66	ACCM contacts +Ely about the proposal from +Portsmouth to allow Cotton to bypass the selection committee and asking, "if you want this reported to the selection committee, or if you think it better that we should say no more about it". *ACCM, clearly concerned, decides to contact +Ely for a "second opinion".*
24 June 66	Response from +Ely: "... of one thing I am quite sure and that is that if +Portsmouth proposes to ordain him, it would be a bad thing for Cotton to tell his story over again with strange people, either at a board or before members of the candidates' committee. So I think the answer is, we should do nothing further about it." *The concern that an ordinand has previously committed a sexual offence against a young person has become lost in the focus on "protecting" Cotton. As a result Cotton did not go through the Church's usual route to training and ordination, which would have provided more objective scrutiny and evaluation of the concerns and possible risks.*

The review concludes:

1. ORDINATION
   The reader will have been struck firstly by the way in which Cotton gained access to the priesthood after having been convicted of a sexual offence against a young person. Cotton was clearly successful at persuading senior figures to support his case for ordination. He was persistent in arguing his cause and, over time, minimised the nature of the incident, denied responsibility for committing it, argued that he pleaded guilty to protect a young person from the need to give evidence, or claimed it was a misunderstanding. His supporters eventually argued the

view that he was "more sinned against than sinner" and that it was "right it be forgotten" and that there could be "a fresh start with ordination". These matters relating to Cotton's ordination were dealt with some 40 years ago and this does need to be kept in mind. However, there was total reliance on Cotton's version of events and no checking of the "source material" by going to the court records. It seems odd that no member of staff from the theological college attended court, heard the verdict and sentence and placed a brief report of Cotton's file. The absence of this allowed Cotton to create a rather different story, which was not challenged. It may be that Cotton did not advise the Theological College staff of his court appearance until after the conviction. What is more difficult to understand [and provide a reasonable explanation of] is why Cotton's case for ordination was promoted in the way it was; such that he was "pushed through" to Theological College the second time without being expected to comply with the usual route of the selection panel and the medical examination. The result was that he was protected from the scrutiny that prospective ordinands would usually receive.

2. SCOUTING AUTHORISATION
The Scout Movement had put a bar on Cotton holding a warrant ever again following his 1954 conviction. Again, Cotton must have persisted in persuading his Diocesan supporters to lobby the Scout Movement, and they eventually agreed to re-license Cotton. This was a significant step as it resulted in Cotton receiving "authorised" and unsupervised access to young people in organised groups. It enabled him to be regarded as an authority figure and a person "of trust" by parents. Many of the situations Cotton's victims talk about or relate to youth activities that Cotton helped organise or led, including abroad."

Eventually, in 2011, the Church of England, in the person of the Bishop of Chichester, accepted responsibility for "mistakes, failures, and lack of knowledge on the part of those who held positions of responsibility ... In the light of his conviction in 1954, Roy Cotton should not have been ordained priest in 1967. Errors of judgment were made about him and his fitness for ministry and ... had the Diocese taken opportunities to investigate his past, the police might have decided to pursue a prosecution prior to his death in 2006."

In her *Report of 19 May 2011*, Baroness Elizabeth Butler-Sloss states:

> "Finally and, in my view, the most important of all his conclusions, he [Roger Meekins] makes the very pertinent point about the effect upon victims who have come forward to give their accounts of abuse suffered by them at the hands of priests within the Diocese. As he says, "The victims were effectively denied the opportunity of being believed in a meaningful sense and denied the opportunity of 'timely' justice. PJ spent many years trying to get the Church [and Sussex Police] to accept his allegations and respond with timely action and recognition of his abuse."

The apology was accompanied by a large sum of compensation for one of his many victims, PJ, who told me (personal conversation, 29 November 2013) in graphic detail how he had been repeatedly raped by Cotton over a ten year period from when he was a young boy. His brother, too, had been raped. Both boys raped by a man who should never have been simply let go by Crookham Court School, never have been welcomed into the Church of England, never have been allowed access to boys.

Mistake piled on mistake to the extent that inconvenient facts were wished away and a dangerous man was allowed unfettered access to his perfect target group.

So in 1961, Robert Smithwick appointed Roy Cotton—a priest, an Oxford graduate, and a convicted sex offender—to the position of joint headmaster of Crookham Court School. He judged that Roy Cotton was the right person for the job. Maybe Robert relied on his judgment alone. As the owner of the school, there was no obligation to ask anyone else's opinion. Had he checked his background, he would have discovered that he was appointing a man with a conviction for a sexual offence. The parents of the children in his care would have an interest in knowing this fact. They were not given the chance to find out. They were let down, but Robert Smithwick himself was dreadfully let down by the Church of England which, two generations later, accepted that he should never have been a priest. So what was particularly attractive about Roy Cotton's candidature for the post?

One of his victims has told me that he was "charming, well-spoken, and well-educated" and that he had "been to Oxford". The official Old Crookhamians website (now taken down) revealed that the school crest was "devised by Roy Cotton" and designed and painted by a parent. It hung in the dining room and bore the motto "Magni Esse Mereamur" (let us deserve to be great). Part of the crest "… depicts an open book resting on sea waves. The book is said to represent Roy Cotton, who gained an MA from Oxford, and the waves represent the naval career of Robert Smithwick, who retained his title of 'Commander'."

Roy Cotton's background was not an open book to Robert Smithwick and, had he known his background, he would not have made an enormous error of judgment in appointing an already convicted abuser, so maybe part of the answer lies in the school register. One of the first pages contains the names of ten boys who joined the school from a school now closed, Lysses School, Fareham. It may be that other pages, now missing, contain more names. The only evidence of the register is a couple of photographs of pages on an old boy's Facebook page. The book itself was destroyed in 2012 by a former teacher, now himself a convicted sex offender, who said its destruction was "on the instructions of the inheritors of the estate". Roy Cotton taught at Lysses School immediately before he started at Crookham Court. So Lysses School appointed a convicted sex offender as a teacher. One of the former pupils, Adam (not his real name), told me how he was abused by Cotton as he lay in his hospital bed after an accident that temporarily robbed him of his sight (personal email, 23 October 2013):

> I was sent by my parents to Lysses School near to Fareham, Hampshire in 1958, they felt the school would give me a better education than the state school I was attending. The first night I was there I was taken from my bed in the dormitory by the house master Cotton to his bedroom where I was stripped, beaten with a cane and sexually assaulted. To say I was terrified would be an understatement. The following morning while in the showers he came to examine my bruised buttocks and when unobserved assaulted me again. This formed the regular pattern of my life for many many months. I believe the Matron whose name I forget did challenge Cotton about the number of times I was being beaten but nothing changed. I can remember one week when I received over 30 strokes of the cane and was assaulted every day. In 1960 Cotton asked my parents if I could be included in an Easter boating holiday trip to the Norfolk Broads. My parents agreed and I was subjected to a ghastly nightly assault for 7 days. I returned to the school totally exhausted. It was impossible to approach my parents who would simply have refused to believe me and most likely punish me. I don't know if Cotton felt he had gone too far but after the Broads trip he did not attack me so much. My time at the school ended not long after when I was shot in the eye by another pupil (accident)

and spent the next 3 years in and out of hospital. On two occasions I was visited in hospital by Cotton. At the time I was completely blind as both my eyes were covered and my head in a block so I could not move. He would sit on the bed and speak to me in a low voice warning what would happen to me if I ever said anything. I have never felt such despair, I was near to death and still this man would not leave me in peace. The story fabricated by the school over what happened blighted my life for years and all I wanted to do was to forget that I had ever seen Lysses and Cotton. I understand the school survived the scandal for some years and during that time Cotton was asked to leave or chose to leave exactly when I don't know.

I do not know where Cotton came from other than he had been studying for the church. As a pupil I would have no idea how he came to be house master or what his qualifications would be. [Name redacted] was the owner of the school and took no interest in its running as far as I experienced. Cotton reappeared by chance for me when I saw an article in a Chichester paper about a paedophile priest and a cover up by the church authorities. The paper printed a picture of the priest and I recognised Cotton at once. I was absolutely horrified when I learned what he had done and to so many people and I shall be sorry for ever for just choosing to ignore what had happened to me and not try to bring him to account.

I do not want to give the impression that these events blighted my life for they did not. I have enjoyed a most wonderful life with my dear wife of 40 years beside me. My working life in Architecture has been a joy and my retirement with my wonderful classic cars has been perfect. It would be a lie if I said that Cotton had not influenced my outlook but as I have always told myself, he did it to me, I am not to blame in any way. That I survived the

> accident is obvious and apart from the loss of sight in one eye the damage done has caused me few problems over the years.

Although justice was not achieved for Adam, nature has taken its course and "the horrid man is dead". He now knows that others suffered at his abuser's hands and did not ignore what had happened to them, that Cotton has been declared in open court to be an abuser linked to a convicted abuser, and the truth is now out.

A survivor and, ultimately, the victor. At a price.

The headmaster who was appointed to replace Roy Cotton, Robby Raven Roberts, wrote to me about Cotton's departure from the headship of Crookham Court (email, 18 May 2011): "The Commander was reticent on the subject. He usually saw what was good in people and was not vindictive. He never offered any particular specifics of Cotton's activities. I believe Cotton was 'let go'."

No record exists to show that the "allegations made or insinuated by boys at the school" were ever reported to any higher authority and there is no record of any reply to the correspondence of the time. Robert Smithwick judged that the man should simply move on; judged that no record be made as to why.

Nowadays checking and reporting are legal requirements. Not so in the 1960s. Another cloud covered a second teacher who left just before I arrived in 1969. He, too, was a priest who "left to revert to the church". He, too, arrived with a number of boys, this time from a school in the West Country that was in a chaotic state with a headmaster who locked himself in his flat and a wife who appeared drunk in front of the boys. An old boy of that school remembered him as a nice man. On that first day I was at Crookham Court School, I noticed a sixteen year old, John, walking around the outside of the building, head down. Day after day at every break he would be there, skulking. Having realised that some of the children who were there had quite special reasons for being away from home, I hesitated to approach him. It was some time before I saw his face clearly. He was good looking and utterly without eye contact. He left after my first term. As he did not do French, I never met him. "He was very upset when Mr. K [not his real initial] left," I was told. Two decades later, without anyone saying a word to me, I had a shrewd idea why Mr. K had left and why John was so withdrawn. There was no follow-up and no counselling, let alone any reporting or prosecution. I do not know what happened to either of them.

Back then, no one assumed the worst. No one suspected. We thought that the teachers were men of good standing and that those who rose to the top must be especially noble. We are now aware, following this and other cases, that motives need to be examined. Whether it is defensible that so much power over children can be concentrated in the hands of one man is also a matter for debate. A board of governors is not a legal requirement. A clever paedophile—and many are—with huge funds—which many have—could today buy a school, inveigle parents, and pay off staff.

While Robert Smithwick would shudder to know what his oversights and too-trusting nature led to with Roy Cotton, he had been let down badly by the Church. Nevertheless, history would repeat itself ten years later and this time it was again a matter of one man's judgment.

FOUR

Those who fail to learn from history are doomed to repeat it

"But I've only got an A Level in it."

It was January 1969. Shafts of winter sun streamed through the grimy windows of "The Study". The headmaster waved his arm expansively, his black gown picking up grains of chalk from the desk and sending them swirling onto the green carpet. "No matter. Just keep a few pages ahead of the boys. They don't know much and you know more than them. You'll do fine. Oh, and maybe you can do some RI, too."

I was shown to a wooden hut in the grounds. A class was assembled there, all in identical blue jumpers. I was briefly introduced, told that all boys were known by their surnames alone, and left to get on with it.

What started as a two-week placement after graduation by the local education office as a "supply teacher" at Crookham Court School to replace its French teacher who had just given birth to a baby, extended into a lifelong connection with a school described in tabloid terms by a Crown Court judge as "a brutal regime" and more colourfully by the tabloids themselves as one of the most notorious schools in Britain.

I had never heard of Crookham Court School before and had no idea what the private school system was about. I had gone from infant to primary to grammar via the 11 Plus—all courtesy of the state.

The twenty-one-year-old me in 1968 armed with an English degree had no idea what he wanted to do. In those days, a passport to a career was a university degree. Not many had one. That qualification was considered to be an indication of intellectual ability, the skills acquired instantly transferable to any profession. To earn some pocket money, I spent that summer doing odd jobs while I thought about what to do. After a few Christmases at the Post Office, I applied for and was given a country route, taking me through the grounds of Highclere Castle, now the "Downton Abbey" of television fame, and out into the sticks. The hum of the wheels of the red and white bike was therapeutic and let me think. There was no hurry. I enjoyed the simplicity of riding, the absence of pressure, the sun on my back. I met the locals when I had a recorded delivery for them. More than one gave me advice on what I should do with my life, surprised that their signature be requested in quite such an RP accent. The late summer wind and rain convinced me that I should seek shelter from the elements while I thought about the future. With no experience of life other than having been taught, I thought I would try my hand at teaching. I put my name down for supply teaching and forgot all about it. A couple of names for reference were requested. I listed my qualifications. No copies of certificates were required and I doubt if my referees were contacted. A few days later, the phone rang. A private boys' school had lost its French teacher to maternity leave and it needed one immediately.

"Good morning. I'll try to pick up from where Mrs. T left you. Shall we have a little chat in French first? So, je dis 'Bonjour' et 'comment appellez-vous?' There was silence. I picked on a sweet-looking blond boy in the front. 'Oui, tu. Ton nom? Tu dois dire 'Mon nom est quelquechose.'" Silence. Another boy put up his hand.

"He's Morrison-Choudhry [not his real name], sir." It was given as an explanation for the silence. Unwisely I persisted. The mouth tightened to a conspicuous closure. I gave him the answer and asked him to repeat it. He burst into tears and rushed from the room. He was the boy who some years later, during a CSE English oral exam was to talk at length about how the buildings at Dulles Airport were more hostile to him than those at Heathrow; the American boy who hated his Indian stepfather, who scratched out the Indian part of his last name, and who was called by the hated name several times a day. I used his first name. He changed.

Although I had no idea at the time, and a realisation of the implications took decades, I had entered what was for some of the children who went there an environment that challenged their lives in the most destructive way imaginable. Crookham Court was a school in which nothing was what it seemed. What I had taken in my naïveté to be a mini public school in the Berkshire countryside, for boys who would achieve more with small classes, was from its inception a magnet for paedophiles with a ready supply of boys handed over by their trusting parents many of whom have no idea to this day what they had, in all innocence, inflicted on their children.

Even the unlikely name "Crookham Court School" has a chill ring. Crook, crooked, not straight, evil, bent, ugly. A lair for monsters, paedophiles, evil seeping from the plaster, the floorboards, the galleried hall. The building, grey, forbidding. What a frightful modern Dotheboys Hall it must have been. Bleak House, grim, gaunt, and outlined on the top of the hill. Its grey slab stone front holding back the swell of terrible secrets bulging in the bare dormitories, hiding in the masters' tiny bedsits. Fetid, lurid, loathsome. That what is good and honest and innocent about childhood has been desecrated there has been proved in court. An affront to education; a gangrene that festered in the cosy world of private schools. In those innocent days of the 1960s when the school was created, childhood was longer and sweeter, yet the evil was there from the start, hidden away and known by just a few. The face Crookham Court presented to the world was happy, ordered, and kind. That was what I saw on that sunny January day in 1969 and it took years for me to be disabused.

Just before my arrival, Robert Smithwick had appointed Robby Raven Roberts as head. "Rave", as he was known with affection, gave the place a touch of the old school. He had come from Addis Ababa via Basingstoke. His Cambridge degree, flowing gown, and fruity vowels gave reassurance of quality. A bon viveur and raconteur, his personality suffused the school. Parents were feted, flattered, and left with the impression that their sons were in the groves of academia, that the cultured erudition emanating from "The Study" and Rave's house, "The Lodge", would be absorbed through the pores. The boys were less convinced. "All piss and no shit" was the succinct considered opinion of one of the sixth-formers.

Robby's daughter, Angela, was there. She was taking examinations prior to going to college. I invigilated her A Levels. It was odd. There were only a couple of years between us. The other staff were older. We became friends and I was a frequent visitor to The Lodge at the other end of the drive from the school building. Dinners there were protracted and vinous, the conversations wide-ranging. Robby's wife, Ann, mini-skirted, kinky-booted, Swedish, and red-haired into her sixties, was a super cook and, when the cupboard was not bare—as it usually was—her hospitality was extended to those few members of staff currently in favour. On a clear summer's evening, her instructions to her daughter, "Anyela, show ze yentlemen into ze yarden," could be heard through the windows of the school down the drive. The dramas and tensions when Rave was beaten around the head with a frozen fish were similarly common knowledge. Much of my education was had over dinner in The Lodge. My throwaway, "Why do you serve a plate on a plate? Is it a quaint old Scandinavian custom?" was seized on with contempt. "Qvaint old Scandinavian custom? Zis is vat comes from not having been to ze best school or Oxford or Cambridge or dining in ze best houses," was her way of hinting to me that one never leaves an empty place in front of a guest. My dropping in through her letterbox the next day an article from a magazine to the effect that a hostess's duty is to make her guest feel welcome and at home went unremarked. My invitations continued, though. "You must write a critique of ze Ballet Rambert for ze magazine." "But I didn't go on that trip." "Vell, at least you vill be unpreyuyiced."

Often unwelcome at home and belaboured by frozen food, Rave was an isolated figure. Staff were picked up and dropped. In and out of his confidence they went. Down the hill to the ford I went in his old blue Vauxhall Victor estate car. "I shouldn't tell you this." Pregnant pause. "In fact, I won't." We drove back.

The teaching was along traditional lines. Some of the staff were well qualified academically, some not. Modern teaching methods hardly applied. On the notice board in Robert's room (the Maths Room) was the admonition, "The Seeds of Education are Bitter, but the Fruit is Sweet". Robert was always "The Commander". He called his staff by surname alone. This was meant kindly. One addressed only tradespeople with the honorific prefix. First names were not relevant here. Boys were surnamed by staff and by each other. Close friends would no more dream of introducing a first name than admitting their affection.

The microcosm of reality that is the world of the small private school took hold. They were all there. The adulterous French teacher, the manic maths master, the lustful, the alcoholic, the derelict, the frustrated. By and large, the boys were educated and such was the sway the Commander held that no one questioned whether modern methods might have been more appropriate. His military training made him appear curt and decisive, as upright as his stance. The boys knew where they stood. They were disciplined. Manners were important. The day was structured and parents left the school to get on with its job. There was little money, but plenty of goodwill. The parents' committee—the "Crookham Court Society"—met a couple of times a term for fund-raising activities and to give the boys treats. Crookham Court appeared to be doing what it had been set up to do. Somewhat shabby and in constant disrepair, no one really minded. Career teachers came and quickly went. Whatever it was that Rave had decided against telling me finally hit home and he left in the summer of 1971.

The veneer of the public school that Rave may have created by way of airs and social graces, his successor, Derek Andrews (not his real name), did not choose to display. A Quaker and a northerner, he looked at the little world he had come to control out of deep-set eyes and rejected its pretensions. Robert was at the stage when he wanted to hand over control of the day-to-day affairs and assume a bursarial role. Derek was the sort of down-to-earth fellow he felt he could leave to get on with it. Married to Charlotte (not her real name) and with two young children, Derek looked at modern methods, suggested that staff should go on courses, introduced a measure of pupil power and, while leaving the ethos of the school undisturbed, set about giving it more relevance to the type of pupil it was seeking to attract. The token sixth form was scrapped. A Level had been expensive in terms of staffing and the success rate was tiny. The traditional O Level courses, while attractive to parents who thought that getting their sons into the O Level stream meant that real progress had been made, were not suitable for those still mastering the basic skills. In came CSE, the watered-down O Level. The remedial side was given more resources. Crookham Court edged forward. Memories of the old "Decline and Fall" days blurred; Robert and Derek achieved a mutual respect; numbers kept up; the years of the early '70s passed.

Cancer came suddenly to Derek Andrews. He felt a slight ache under his arm while driving the boys to an archery match in the minibus one Sunday afternoon. He found the lump that he thought was the cause and went to the doctor without delay. Test followed test. His decline was swift. From being a sporty six-footer in his mid-thirties, within a year he was on his back in hospital. His mind keen, alert, articulate. His body deteriorating, useless, skeletal. The irony was not lost on him. He was not a man to complain, but he resented his inexorable decay. "It's all right here." He pointed to his head. "It's just that I can't do anything with this." He lifted his arm to indicate the him that lay on the bed. This was the first and only time that he came close to mentioning the inevitability of his death or of giving in to despair. Everything thenceforth was unsaid. It was unmentionable. It covered everything with its grey horror, but was never remarked on. It just was. There would be no escape. It was the elephant in the room and it was all so unfair. Illness had never before intruded into Derek's life. He never smoked, hardly ever drank, was not one to feel stress, had a wife and two small children, was active, happy, and positive about what he was doing. His body was crumbling and he could see it.

Even more cruel was the remission. For just a few weeks, he returned home and came into the school. We were seduced by hope. Within the month he was dead.

For Robert, this was the start of real problems. He had come to depend on Derek. The parts of the running of the school that Robert had no interest in were now his burden. It was just work. The financial reward was negligible. Robert's wife, Rosemary, had died in December 1969. The date remains clear in my mind. It was the night of the Christmas dinner. Someone joked that from the thirteen of us sitting down to dinner on the 13th, one would not make it through the night. She was taken to hospital with double pneumonia just after the meal and died in the early hours. The grip Robert had on his emotions was as tight as his clenched fist that morning. "Let the parents know the Carol Service has been cancelled and that they can come and collect the boys when they wish." "Is there anything else we can do?" Angela and I asked. "That's kind, but no." "Can we take the boys out somewhere?" "No, I like to have them here."

We interpreted loneliness as self-sufficiency. Robert had never made an art out of expressing feelings. We had come to think of him as not possessing them. Shortly after her husband's death, Derek's widow, Charlotte, phoned me. It was after midnight and she needed to talk. "He proposed to me." "Who?" "Robert." "What did you say?" "I said no. It's just too soon. He said that he couldn't run the school on his own." It was that brief. For a moment a possible future for Crookham Court School had flickered. It was all a matter of judgment again. His timing was hopeless. The flame was snuffed out and in that moment another future for Crookham Court was emerging.

Bernard Stone (not his real name) was appointed headmaster by Robert. He was more in the public school mould, wished to be addressed as "Headmaster" and had some of the delusions that we thought had disappeared with Rave. It was 1977, the year of the Silver Jubilee. It was a time for celebration, but for Crookham Court it was the point at which everything changed. A few weeks after rejecting Robert, Charlotte had taken up with a male member of staff. Within a few months, they were married. The Crookham Court Society sensed that Robert was disenchanted with Crookham. He had said more than once that if someone made him an offer, he would sell. We had not believed it then, but we believed it now. The idea of a purchase was raised. Several of the parents could have afforded it, but before a plan could be drawn up, Robert announced that he had sold the school.

I had a hint of this a few weeks earlier from Charlotte. "He's seen an advertisement. Someone is advertising to buy a school.

He told me not to say anything, so you mustn't, but he's found a buyer." I kept my word and told no one.

Robert was guarded about his successor. "I've made way for an older man," he said. "He plans to take a back seat in the running of the school and will have a different style from mine." Robert was always terse, but the staff were curious. After all, they and the boys had been sold along with the school and everything in it. "He has been invited to Speech Day, but is rather shy and has declined." We wanted to meet him, to get the measure of him—this man who was to take us over. All we found out before the start of the autumn term in 1977 was his name. Philip Cadman.

Robert took up no references about Cadman. Had he done so, he would have found that he had taught at many schools and that he had been dismissed from most. He might also have found that he had abused a child at a school he was teaching at in 1959. But Robert never asked. Was it that he assumed the man's motives must have been laudable because he was in the teaching profession, or was it that he was on the rebound and wanted to get shot of the school quickly, or did he just not bother? Whatever the reason, Robert Smithwick exercised his judgment once again to take a man at face value and did not understand or overlooked or—whoops—just didn't spot what was clear to all of us within minutes of meeting him, that there was something about this man that was very odd.

FIVE

The art of buying loyalty

Captain Saumarez Philip Cadman showed his face to those he had bought at Crookham Court School on the first day of the autumn term, 11 September 1977. Parents were milling around, unpacking their sons' trunks, boys were greeting friends, the Crookham Court Parents' Society was meeting in the library and there was Cadman, apparently unaware of what this bustle of activity around him meant. Mouth slightly ajar, a downward look, an expression of puzzlement, quite at a loss what to say. He said little to anyone. I doubt if most of the parents seeing him in the main hall realised that he owned it. That he also owned everyone in it was soon to become clear.

It was the slippers that made me realise that whatever else he might be, this man was not charismatic. The brown-check, fleece-lined velour bedroom slippers. The ultimate incongruity on the first day of term. Parents, teachers, pupils, principal—and principal's slippers. Was I the only one to notice? I thought of *The Emperor's New Clothes*. The emperor was wearing slippers and no one was pointing the finger, no one was laughing. "Err, good afternoon," was just about all he could mutter. His small eyes skittered in their dark sockets, looking at the floor. His discomfiture was all too obvious. Yet people wanted to listen to him, to pay attention to him. A modest man, I wondered? No, it's more complicated than this. He must have known what taking on a school would be like. A shy man who had paid the purchase price to be principal, to be the one at the top, and who had no social skills, let alone leadership? Nothing squared. Perhaps he would take a back seat as Robert had said. I dismissed the thought. He was at the same time out of his element, but relishing it. He remained; a fixture in the library. He wanted to be part of this scene. It was his play, his theatre, his starring role and he held it in his clenched fists.

The minutes of the parents' meeting, the Crookham Court Society, on 10 September 1977 make no mention of the arrival of a new owner. The rose garden that had been planted some months before in memory of Derek Andrews had died. £72.25 was needed to replant it. The society agreed to finance this and I was asked to arrange it. The suggestion was made that a portrait of the Commander be commissioned as a retirement present and that it be placed in the vestibule. This was duly agreed and £125 of society funds was set aside for this. "The chairman thanked his committee and all the members and parents who had supported him during the last year and by their efforts had benefited their children and others in the years to come." It was proposed that the chairman was to become a life member of the society. This was carried unanimously. The new chairman took over. Parents and staff were proposed, seconded, and agreed. The Christmas Fair was planned. It was suggested that parents be asked to give two books of Green Shield stamps in order to exchange them for gifts for the tombola stall. The meeting closed at 7.45 pm. The glorious early autumn afternoon outside; the aroma of floor polish inside. My unease at what I had sensed in the hall remained unspoken. The idyllic times were just about to end.

During the days immediately afterwards, the staff were prepared to say to each other that something was wrong. No one was yet willing to acknowledge that the emperor had no clothes, but this lay at the heart of everyone's concern. I was reminded of W. H. Auden's lines: in "Epitaph on a Tyrant":

> He knew human folly like the back of his hand …
> When he laughed, respectable senators burst with laughter,
> And when he cried the little children died in the streets.

Cadman knew exactly what he was doing. He was a sharp operator, underestimated by everyone. All the power was his. All the players were in his pay. All the children were in what passed for his care.

Bernard Stone, the headmaster Robert had appointed and sold to Cadman, had on the first afternoon been accused by Cadman of stealing a cheque. That it had appeared in Cadman's desk drawer shortly afterwards had elicited little by way of apology. Most staff treated Cadman with due deference. He paid the salaries. The staff relied on them.

The boys were less circumspect. Two days into that first week, relations were breaking down. Cadman's subject was maths. At first, he was being yelled at in the classroom and around the school. The boys then realised that they could punch him as he passed, with impunity, and cut pieces out of his gown. One pinned a scrap of paper to it with "I'M A THICKIE" in capital letters. The staff met in the English Room, my classroom, one lunchtime. What could be done? What sort of man was he? The man was a disciplinary disaster and, while every school carries one or two, he was the school. There was unanimity. We had only been there a few minutes when Cadman sidled into the room. He had heard there was a meeting. He knew intrigue was afoot. Everything we needed to discuss was there. The moment to point or even to start laughing had arrived. No one spoke. The moment passed. The meeting terminated quickly and the staff left, requesting a full staff meeting.

This was held on 16 September 1977. The minutes are couched in the language of diplomacy:

The Headmaster said that the staff were very worried about the School and asked the Principal to clarify certain points. Bernard Stone asked Cadman what he considered the role of the Headmaster to be. Cadman said he considered that students and staff should be recruited by the Principal, Headmaster and staff in consultation and that the final decision would lie with the Principal. It was said the staff felt that the Headmaster should decide on acceptance. The Principal said that discipline was the responsibility of the Headmaster and that he (the Principal) must have people who were going to co-operate with him. It was mentioned that the Headmaster had the full support of the Crookham Court Society and the staff.

The Headmaster asked the Principal what he considered the role of the Principal to be. The Principal said he was not prepared to commit himself in advance. It was asked that if problems arose, to whom were the staff to go. The Principal said that the Headmaster would deal with the day-to-day running of the School and that he (the Principal) would have the final veto.

The Principal was asked if he had formed ideas on the level of Mathematics in the School. He said that it was difficult to teach boys who did not want to learn. He was asked if the School was to keep these boys. He said that it might be necessary to keep them for the sake of the continuity of the School. The Staff mentioned that some of the boys did not know who the Principal was and that it was necessary for the Principal to have good discipline. The Principal said he was loath to expel boys. He was informed that on a previous occasion, a boy had been expelled for threatening a member of staff with physical assault and was asked if this would now be grounds for expulsion. The Principal said that it depended on the boy, that it would not necessarily follow and that it depended on considerations such as the number of boys in the

School at the time. He pointed out that it was not unusual for staff to be assaulted in comprehensive schools.

Throughout, the terms were measured and guarded. What was screaming to be said, was not said. Cadman's will would prevail whatever the staff thought. He knew it. Doddery and dotty he may have appeared, but he had an absolute mastery of human frailty. Within the week he had neutralised whatever threat the staff might pose.

Under the headmaster as senior master was the chaplain, a man Derek Andrews had told me he would not wish to have at his death bedside. He was away recuperating at the start of term and came in after the staff meeting. As school secretary was Derek's widow, soon to have another name.

By early October, the friction between Bernard Stone and Cadman was obvious. Stone could see that Cadman was destroying whatever discipline he was trying to enforce and at the same time was criticising him for the lack of it around the school. Boys were running in and out of the Maths Room windows during lessons. On the old "Fruits of Education …" notice were scrawled graffiti. The walls were spattered with pellets. On a daily basis, Cadman would run the gauntlet of insults, swearing, taunts, and blows. For him, this was the norm. These were his pupils. Boys will be boys. They were becoming besotted with their power. They could do what they liked. Many of them loved it. Others were almost weeping with frustration. None could learn. Punishments were given at random and the staff had the task of seeing they were done. It was all a nonsense. I thought Cadman would be lucky to last the term. In fact, he lasted another twelve years. What follows is how he did it.

By early October, Bernard Stone could stand no more. He and the Crookham Court Society met at my home and drafted "The Headmaster's Minimum Requirements" (later appended to the minutes of a "Meeting held in the Carnarvon Room at the Chequers Hotel on Sunday October 30th 1977"). They were perfectly sensible:

1. The Principal to be responsible for the financial aspects of Crookham Court Limited.
2. The Headmaster to work within the Principal's financial allowance.
3. The Headmaster to have control of student intake according to policy laid down previously by Principal, Headmaster and staff according to contracts agreed by parents.
4. The Headmaster to have complete control of discipline. The Headmaster would not expel without consultation, but would expect his decision to be agreed with. Financial considerations would not apply to expulsions.
5. The Headmaster to have complete control over the day-to-day running of the School.
6. The Headmaster to have complete control over the teaching.
7. The Headmaster to have complete control over the social side of the School.
8. The Headmaster to have complete control over the social welfare of the boys.
9. It would be the Headmaster's responsibility to appoint staff with the Principal's agreement.
10. The ultimate control of staff to lie with the Headmaster.
11. The Headmaster to be the direct line of communication with parents on all matters with the exception of Fees.

Logical they might be. Appealing to a multimillionaire who was the king of the castle he had always wanted to be, they were not. Cadman rejected them out of hand. Stone resigned. The chairman of the Crookham Court Society wrote to all the parents (letter, 24 October 1977):

> It has been brought to my attention as Chairmen of the Crookham Court Society that the Headmaster,

> Mr. Bernard Stone, has given notice of his intention to vacate his position at the end of the Spring Term or earlier by arrangement. As a parent or guardian of a boy at present attending the School, I feel you will receive this news with mixed feelings and would, therefore, like clarification of the present and future position. To write and explain the circumstances under which Mr. Stone is leaving is difficult, so I am calling a Meeting of the Crookham Court Society at 6.45 pm on Sunday, 30 October. I trust you will make every effort to attend this Meeting.

There was a postscript:

> When I approached Mr. Cadman for permission to hold the above Meeting last Saturday, I was refused. Today I received a letter of confirmation, also a standard letter sent to all parents. In this letter he asks for the Society to be disbanded. This I feel he does not have the right to do. So please make every effort to attend the Meeting arranged for 7.30 pm on Sunday 30 October at the Chequers Hotel, Newbury. The full facts as known will be placed before you at this Meeting and any action will be yours to take.

Cadman had beaten him to it. Not only had he acquired a new secretary, the former head's wife, but he also had a new acting headmaster, the recently-returned chaplain, waiting in the wings. He had written to all the parents (letter dated 22 October 1977):

> A few weeks after the beginning of this term, I was presented with a document entitled "Minimum Requirements of the Headmaster" by members of the Crookham

> Court Society and I was requested to sign it. In default of which the Headmaster threatened to resign and a full meeting of the Society would be summoned for half term at which further action would be discussed. As the owner and Chairman of Crookham Court Limited, I was not prepared to sign a document containing 13 demands which would have virtually taken all control of the School out of my hands and merely left me with the power to sign the cheques. I explained this to the members of the Society and I had the impression that they understood my point-of-view. Since then the Headmaster, Mr. Stone, has tendered his formal resignation. I believe a full meeting of the Crookham Court Society and parents has been arranged for Sunday 30 October. I do not believe that this Meeting will be in the best interests of the School or myself. I have therefore decided, after consultation, to disband the Crookham Court Society forthwith and to cancel the planned Meeting. The Christmas Fair has also been cancelled.
>
> It is with considerable regret that I have felt compelled to take this action, but I consider it in the best interests of the School.
>
> I hope the parents will continue to support the School as they have always done in the past. The present Headmaster, Mr. Stone's, resignation dates from the end of April 1978. I shall take every step to replace him with a man worthy of the position.

Headmaster out, parents banned, even Christmas cancelled. All was within his power. It never occurred to me that the parents would stand for it. They met to discuss and, in effect, accepted the fait accompli. The minutes of that meeting, held in the Carnarvon Room at the Chequers Hotel on Sunday 30 October 1977, are garbled, but convey the real concerns parents were feeling.

Letters were read out … . Minutes of the 16 September Staff Meeting were read out.

[And then—] Mr. Cadman joined the Meeting at this stage together with X, Y and Z (teachers). The parents were invited to put questions to Mr. Cadman.

One parent suggested that the points disagreed between Mr. Cadman and Mr. Stone should be read out there and then for Mr. Cadman's comments. Another asked for assurances that the School would be allowed to continue as before and that the small classes and good tuition be allowed to remain. It was stressed by another parent that after 18 months without a Headmaster a good man had now been found and that his resignation would ruin the chances of the boys.

Mr. Cadman reverted to the financial situation of the School. He stated that he did not know this until two weeks before term had started.

A parent asked if it was possible to have a stable staff for one year. Boys sitting exams were going to suffer. She also asked if more changes were expected and how Mr. Cadman expected to run the School without parental support.

It was suggested that a practical way to resolve the difficulties was for there to be a Board of Governors.

References about Mr. Cadman which had been heard were disturbing and one parent stated that as the School was being run unsuccessfully he would remove his boy if nothing were done.

Mr. Cadman replied that Mr. Stone had tendered his resignation which had been accepted. The Chaplain would be taking over as Headmaster. The School would go on as before.

Mr. X said that after four years at the School, he was 100% behind Mr. Cadman. The Chaplain said he supported Mr. Cadman 100%.

> The Chairman asked Mr. Cadman if he would consider selling the School. Mr. Cadman asked how much was being offered.

A sub-committee was instituted to explore this possibility, but Cadman had no intention of selling. He had staff on his side and this was some reassurance to parents. There was an element of continuity. Cadman's allies had given him credibility.

The damage had been done. The chance had been missed. Cadman held sway.

Cadman could have been stopped by the parents on that day. Twelve years later, it was a child who did that.

Bernard Stone continued as head for some weeks. The Christmas dinner to which we were traditionally invited by the principal was a dismal affair. After the meal, coffee was served in the staff common room. As it was being served, Cadman took the opportunity of the festive occasion to announce that with immediate effect he was dismissing Bernard Stone for disloyalty. It was quite matter-of-fact. "Gross disloyalty to me and the school," he grunted. Cadman wanted to impress us with the juxtaposition. That it was, perhaps, questionable taste for the host to choose a social function to sack one of his guests was easy to dismiss as another unfortunate solecism from one who had dismissed the parents, disgraced the teaching profession, and thrown an entire school into disharmony. Conversation became a touch stilted after this. Bernard Stone made his excuses and left the room. He became a non-person. Contractually he was allowed to remain in his home, The Lodge at the end of the drive, but anyone asking for him was told he had left. The chaplain took over as head; others gave him support.

The "disloyalty" that had so affronted Cadman had been getting references on him. Bernard Stone had been asking around. It was his undoing that his calls on the school telephone system could be listened into. There had been several previous employers who had been less than satisfied with

Cadman. Even the local grammar school in Newbury had sacked him. Those prepared to comment informally were not prepared to commit their thoughts to paper. Had they done so, a pattern would have been seen at that time. He had left a number of schools—possibly thirteen of them according to the rumour doing the rounds—under a cloud. It had been a similar cloud each time.

Bernard and Margaret Stone continued to live in The Lodge throughout the spring term of 1978. They never appeared in the school. Boys continued to be recruited. The chaplain took over as the acceptable face of Crookham Court School, interviewing parents and boys. Cadman had two posts to fill. One term of him was enough for me. I handed in my resignation (by letter, 6 January 1978): "I wish to terminate my employment with Crookham Court Limited at the end of this term (18 March 1978). In accordance with professional procedure, I am giving a term's notice."

He could not find a replacement head of English. The only one who applied, he told me, was Bill Dexter (not his real name). "A rough diamond" was Cadman's comment. Frequently red-faced and rolling drunk, Bill Dexter was a gentleman; a character straight out of *Decline and Fall*. At Crookham, he found a home, kids to entertain, and companions to drink with. He joined the English department. I returned at Cadman's request, part-time. My aim would be to close the place down. It was not an aim I found possible to disclose to any of the staff. I did not need the income teaching brought in. They did. In light of this, that they were, eventually, to go as far as they did in bringing the nonsense that was Crookham Court to the attention of the authorities was laudable. Had they resigned en masse at the outset, twelve years of chaos would have been avoided.

Finding a headmaster was not difficult. The man chosen was a non-graduate. To be propelled suddenly into the stratosphere, to attain the dizzy height of headmaster of Crookham

Court without even a degree, was a dream. Throughout the twelve years of Cadman's reign, he had six headmasters. He believed that heads were there to do as they were told and if they didn't do that, they were sacked. Most of them left before he had the chance to deliver the final blow. The first one lasted longest, staying in harness for a full four years, giving Cadman apparently complete support. By the time he left he had few illusions about him. At one of the last staff meetings he chaired, Cadman left for a phone call. It had been a fraught affair. One of the boys was running a soft drinks business and keeping the profit. Indeed, he was so privileged as to be beyond the normal range of punishments for failing to attend lessons. Cadman was not concerned about his money-making and seemed to admire his spirit. The staff found this favouritism gross and, in that they had come to tolerate most of Cadman's nonsense, had been raising muted and oblique objections to this. The minutes were suspended in Cadman's absence. I took the opportunity to say to the head, "Do you really think Mr. Cadman has the sense of moral responsibility to be in charge of children?" He looked at me squarely from behind his thick glasses, his eyes enlarged and intent. "No," he said quietly. I believe he meant it.

By the end of his first term, Cadman had already shown his ability to sail through the most surreal situations. I arrived one Sunday morning to find a police car at the front door. One of the staff, David Matthews (not his real name), was waiting in the hall, flushed with anger. "What is it now?" "Cadman's called the police. He said an attempt was made to assassinate him last night." It seems that he had been working late in the main study on the ground floor when a bullet was fired at the window. Cadman threw himself to the floor and crawled under the desk. He had remained there for some time before sensing that his attacker had left, and going to bed. When asked why he had not called the police at that time, he replied that he had not wished to disturb them. He had left 100 sleeping boys to the mercy of a crazed gunman in the bushes and gone to bed. When he decided to involve the law next morning, he asked the boys to get Mr. Stone and Mr. Matthews and ask them to bring their guns. The boys loved the intrigue. Did their new principal suspect that their teachers, his own staff, were trying to murder him? Had they not realised from day one that this man's hold on reality was tenuous, they would have been frightened. Even Cadman may have had his doubts. When the police asked him if he had any enemies, he had replied, "Yes. The parents."

No bullet was ever found. The mark in the glass bore all the signs of a stone having come from a catapult.

The boys knew that it took little to precipitate these situations. The secretary came to him one afternoon to say that she had just put the phone down from a call saying there was a bomb in the school. Some minutes later, the matron asked him why he was standing outside. "Don't go in," he warned her. "There's a bomb in there."

The boys may not have been frightened, but I was. Being a bad teacher and not having any form of authority over the boys were not, in themselves, insuperable problems. One assumed that the principal of a school would possess qualities of leadership and control and that his positioning himself at the top of a school would be a way for him to exercise such skills. In Cadman's case, he employed other people to fill these functions. What worried me was that he believed he was in control. He wished to take control. He presented himself as the ultimate authority. He would overrule any of his staff without hesitation. Boys would be taken out of bed to receive phone calls. They would be late with impunity if they had "been with the principal". Punishments would be rescinded. Favours would be bestowed. He had no conception that he was damaging children's lives; that the stability that children expected from those in authority was being presented to them in a distorted form.

Some of the nonsense was funny. In 1980, there was an exchange of correspondence on the notice board. Cadman's note (dated 5 June 1980) read:

> To All Concerned.
>
> In the past it has been the custom to give a cricket ball or other material award to a boy who distinguished himself at cricket by making a large score or taking a certain number of wickets.
>
> Over the past two years I have experienced on frequent occasions rudeness and a lack of co-operation on the sports field.
>
> For this reason I have decided to discontinue the award of a cricket ball to the batsman who makes 50 runs, but hope that the satisfaction of making a good score for your side will prove a sufficient incentive.—S. P. Cadman.

A reply from one of the boys was instant. Posted on the board the same day came the following:

> Dear Mr. Cadman,
>
> With reference to your letter dated 5.6.80 posted in the lobby about the presentation of cricket balls to students scoring more than 50 runs, we would like to state the following.
>
> As it is obvious that you are in grave financial difficulties, the school has decided to purchase a cricket ball to be presented on your behalf to M.H. on Speech Day. We wish to point out that, should there be any future difficulties in the maintenance of established and worthwhile school traditions, we would appreciate your mentioning this in confidence to your prefects.
>
> We would like to assure you of our continued loyalty to you and the school—a loyalty which would stretch, if necessary, to our last new penny.
>
> Yours most faithfully, etc.

Some of it was not funny. A few days after this the art teacher was beaten by a boy with a hockey stick. Indiscipline was becoming the norm. I wrote a memo to the head (dated 13 June 1980):

> As you know, I showed one of the BBC's "Life on Earth" series to an assortment of the 4th Form this afternoon.
>
> I was treated to a display of ill-manners which is, I gather, becoming quite common in the school, but which I have not as yet experienced in this direct way. Before the boys entered the room, they were swearing at each other, using the most objectionable words and shoving each other out of the way to find a seat.
>
> During the film, [names radacted] in particular tried to be as disruptive as possible. After the film, no one bothered to express any thanks.
>
> I do not think this display was unconnected with Wednesday's events. If the pupils can see another pupil go unpunished after beating a member of staff with a hockey stick, we all become vulnerable. I find the present lack of discipline among the boys and the amount of bullying and aggression taking place daily, quite frightening. The staff need the support of the study in ending the violence and abuse. The study must make it clear that such behaviour cannot be tolerated and must act promptly. Very positive steps must be taken. It may already be too late.'

No form of support or recognition was forthcoming. The head's memo in reply came the next day (14 June 1980):

> I am sorry to hear that you were not pleased with the behaviour of the fourth year boys yesterday.
>
> You appear to have overheard boys swearing, and watched or heard them shoving each other out of the way.

> You surely corrected their behaviour whilst queuing? Allowed them into the room in an orderly manner, insisted they were attentive and corrected their lack of courtesy in not expressing their thanks at the end?
>
> If you did none of these things then I would say this is precisely one of the reasons for your general complaint and I would expect you to follow it up today. If you did take appropriate action throughout then I assume your memo is for information only.
>
> Whilst the conclusion to Wednesday's events may not be to your satisfaction (although I would point out you are not in full possession of all the facts) it simply reinforces the need for each teacher to respond to each situation as it occurs as effectively as he can and should be able to do.
>
> The implication of your memo is that you said or did nothing—this does not help anyone.

Problem neatly resolved and no need to do anything. The member of staff whacked with the hockey stick left, the boy carried on at the school and his parents continued to pay the fees. Staff came and went. Even the chaplain had had enough and took over a parish.

By the following year most of the staff instrumental in backing Cadman at the 1977 Parents Meeting had gone. New staff were beginning to raise questions. Part of the minutes of a staff meeting on 27 April 1981 indicates their concern as a backdrop to what was about to happen. Questions were put by the new chaplain in his capacity of union (Assistant Masters and Mistresses Association) representative:

> Everyone was very concerned with the smooth running of the school and the well-being of the pupils and that for this reason any problems or ideas should be brought out into the open and discussed in an adult and

amicable manner without clashes of personality. Also it was imperative that anything said within the four walls of the staff room should remain confidential and a united front be displayed to the boys. ... A point was raised in connection with unprofessional conversations with boys. Several staff had instances to relate of remarks made by boys with the inference that unprofessional comments had been made to boys. It was felt that personal matters connected with staff salaries, should remain confidential at all times. The staff endeavour to adhere to certain standards of professional behaviour and would like Mr. Cadman to do likewise.

Mr. Cadman replied that he did not discuss personal matters with boys, but it was possible that if he left the room, boys could look at confidential information.

The staff would also appreciate it if Mr. Cadman did not have confrontations with them in corridors and in front of boys as this is also unprofessional practice. The Principal, Headmaster and staff should present a united front in order to maintain discipline. The Chaplain pointed out that the school had rules for silent reading. These rules had on various occasions been broken by Mr. Cadman himself.

The third point raised by the staff was did Mr. Cadman think that the bad discipline and vandalism was directly related to his own problem of maintaining discipline inside and outside the classroom? To which Mr. Cadman replied that he did not think so.

A memo dated 20 May 1980 stated:

Mr. Cadman requested the following to be added to the Minutes of the last meeting with reference to the questions asked by the Union to the Principal: "In a conversation with a boy about the Principal, a member of staff was told

> by a boy that the Principal had been sacked 17 times. The honourable member then thought fit to ask the Principal if this was true. I replied it was not true and another member of staff asked if it was true that the Principal had been sacked 16 times. The answer was again that it was not true. I think that this should be added to the records so we get a correct picture of the staff meeting."

Staff came, took their money and most left after a short stay. A few long-serving teachers remained, maybe in the hope that somehow things would improve, maybe out of a sense of responsibility for the children's well-being, or possibly out of inertia.

My view at the time was that only if all Cadman's staff left en masse, leaving the children with Cadman in sole charge of them would "the authorities" have been precipitated into action. Would this have been a responsible course of action? Would the teachers have been accused of a dereliction of duty? The moral dilemma was never addressed. "I've got mouths to feed," was the answer I received when I made the suggestion.

SIX

The tormented and the tormentors

If things were bad for the staff, they were worse for some of the boys.

A personal message came through on Facebook (19 May 2012). At his request, I have used Matthew Gray's real name and words: "Hello, Mr. Mucklejohn, I don't know whether you remember me, M. J. Gray, but I went to that Hell-hope, CC, between '78-'82 it's good to see you on facebook after all this time. Maybe we could meet and catch-up."

We exchanged Facebook messages that day: "I've been wracking my brain, but you'll be fixed in my memory as your 16 year-old self. Hell hope or hellhole? It all changed in 1977 and what a dreadful place it became. I assume you've dipped into the CC FB page and maybe the Survivors of CC page. Do you want to skype me? My skype identity is v … ."

"Yes I went into CC FB and the Survivors of CC page. It has brought-up alot of nasty memories. Memories I would rather forget, but now it is time to face my demons."

"OK, Matthew," I replied. "I think you want to tell me what happened to you. Please feel you can go ahead in complete confidence. How do you want to move forward? Would you like to come and see me?"

On 6 June 2012, he left this message on the Crookham Court Facebook page: "My name is Matthew Gray and I spent 4 years of HELL in Crookham Court Boarding School. With all due respect, no amount of medication will counter-act what some of us went though. I see you are friends with Andy Hudson and Ian Mucklejohn. Ian was my English teacher and he was one of the nicest teachers at the school."

A few days before this, I had collected him at the station. Matthew Gray was forty-seven. He looked sixty. He was haunted, gaunt, wary. The following exchanges are from our conversation on 29 May 2012: "It was every day." He paused and looked me in the eye. "Every day. For four years. I was beaten, kicked and tormented. I had TCP poured down my throat in the dormitory by the dorm prefect who told me I snored. Sometimes he would soak a cloth in TCP and put it over my nose and mouth. I'd wake up choking. When I went to bed, I didn't know how I'd wake up.

"They sent me to that place. My parents. They just wanted me away from them. I begged them to take me away from there when I first arrived at Crookham Court, but they wouldn't."

"Did you tell them what was happening to you?"

"Wouldn't've made a difference. They didn't like me. They wanted me to be a failure. They humiliated me at home, so when I went to Crookham it was more of the same. Every day it would be a dead arm or a dead leg or a punch. They called me 'Gay Gray'. That was my name. 'Gay Gray'. All the time. Can you imagine what it felt like in a boys' school? It was every day. It never stopped."

"Are there incidents that stick in your mind?"

There was no pause for thought. Whatever had happened to Matthew may have been buried deep inside, but now it was right on the tip of his tongue. "One day two of them tied a rope around my wrists. They dragged me through the grounds round the side of the school and then they climbed up one of those really big redwood trees in the woods. They must've gone up forty feet. They pulled the rope over one of the huge branches and hauled me up."

"Didn't you yell for them to stop?"

"'Course I did. Made no odds. They kept pulling and I went up. Then they let the rope go. I just fell to the ground. They ran off laughing."

Matthew paused. "I told a couple of the boys who didn't bully me what had happened, but there wasn't any point in complaining to the staff. The boys were doing what they wanted. The only time I complained it got back to the bullies and they laid into me."

There was more. It was as if he was not talking about himself, but another Matthew Gray: one who had lived some time ago and who had been a frightened child. The fear had been replaced by a coldness, a watchfulness that spoke of years of self-reliance and an absence of trust. It seemed that so long ago that I no longer remembered the circumstances, I had taken his sixteen-year-old self to one side, asked him what was wrong, and told the then headmaster that he was being bullied and by whom. The perpetrators of that incident were punished and for that reason Matthew felt able to open up to me. More than thirty years later, he would articulate the details to me.

"You were part-time, not there at the weekends. It was worse then. It was a Saturday afternoon. There wasn't anything on. Most of the boys were out in Thatcham or Newbury. Three of them grabbed me. There was Dan James [not his real name] and Pete Symons [not his real name] and someone else. I can't remember. They grabbed me after lunch in the tiled hall just off the theatre and dragged me to the showers. They held me down and stripped off my sweater and T-shirt and unzipped my jeans. They pulled them off me until I was just in my underpants and socks. Then they got out a rope. They tied my wrists together and tied the other end to the shower head. When I was up there with my arms in the air, they had a pair of leads with bare wires on one end and electrodes on the other. They put the electrodes on my nipples."

Matthew's eyes had steadily met mine throughout. He was calmly matter-of-fact. What he was telling me had been sitting inside his head for three decades, unspoken. He had lived and relived these moments uncountable times.

"When they'd done that, they pulled off a metal plate that was covering a socket and touched the bare wire to the mains. Twice they did it. Just for a second, but I've never felt pain like it. Have you ever been electrocuted? It was the worst pain.

"Then they jerked the electrodes off my nipples. They didn't unclip them, they just pulled. They were so sore from the shocks that I didn't feel it, but I should have. They untied me and I fell down in a heap.

"When they had gone, laughing and shouting, I picked up my clothes, put them on and went into the woods. I just wanted to go somewhere I could be alone.

"It was every day. Every day."

"Matthew, this was premeditated. They had everything arranged. Lined up. All the equipment."

"Yes, I s'pose so. I hadn't thought about it until just now, but yes."

"Gentleness, tenderness ... there wasn't any of that in your life, Matthew, was there?"

These concepts were not part of this man's currency. His life at Crookham Court had been wretched and did not get much better when he left—unable to relate to others, always watching out for an attack, anticipating the cruelty that had become his daily lot.

"I couldn't keep up relationships. Couldn't get on with other people. And women might as well be on another planet. And, yes, I thought about ending it. I came that close. Eventually I was on the streets. I was homeless and lived in a bandstand at night. Sleeping on concrete is cold and horrible, but I was free."

Matthew paused. He had given up feeling anything.

"You've become desensitised, Matthew. That's what they've done to you. Rather than feel anything, you feel nothing now. That's no way to live. You deserve better. One thing has struck me in all the awful things I've been hearing and that is that talking about it really helps. Not just talking around the subject, but letting it all hang out. Another boy has told me everything. Every detail. He told me how his body reacted when he was abused sexually. He kept nothing hidden and it was a relief, such a relief when he had said it all. The sky hadn't fallen in, the sun still shone, and the world still turned after he had told me what had been eating him up for all those years, decades. And he knew that he still had my respect. He could hold his head high. Don't be hard on yourself, Matthew."

"But it's not those boys I blame. I don't blame them. Things happened to them, too. They were just kids. It's the school I blame."

"This is what happens when the normal order of things breaks down. Cadman hardly bought the school to give children a wonderful and developmental experience, did he? But that's what education should be about. You had none of this. There was no moral leadership or guidance. The lunatic really was running the asylum. You had the opposite of what you should have had. Your childhood was just messed up. As were all the children who went there. Will you let me report this to the police?"

Matthew agreed and from that moment it was out of my hands.

Among the boys that he had identified, a name stood out. One day, two years before, he had walked out of his house leaving his wife and young children, stood on the railway line, and ended his life.

One of the more successful old boys put some messages on the Crookham Court Facebook page after Matthew's, telling those who had suffered abuse that they should accept that it was part of the public school system and get over it.

Matthew, his tormentors, and the boy who told him to get over it had all been brutalised by a regime in which physical abuse and absence of human feeling became the norm.

For teachers who were essentially decent and well-intentioned people, what they were seeing every day was nowhere near everyday for them. How can a rich man get any pleasure from being tormented every day by children and questioned all the time by staff? Never was the idea mooted that there might be a sexual element to this. Cadman was elderly, not particularly fussy about his personal hygiene and decidedly lacking in charisma. It was not possible to imagine anyone getting close to him. The issue was the example he was setting and the undesirable effect this had on the developing mind and the fact that children's education was being mismanaged. Sexual abuse was never even thought of as a motive, yet it underpinned everything.

SEVEN

The impotence of "the authorities"

My feeling that something was wrong and that Cadman needed to be stopped had always to be suffixed with "stopped from doing what?".

It was the "what?" that I had the greatest difficulty with. What was it that made an unlikely person like Cadman take over a school that was falling to pieces, with staff who loathed him, children who disrespected him daily, and chaos all round him? In the '70s and '80s, what is so obvious to us now did not occur to any of us. I have no guilt that I did not spot it. Like almost everyone else, I was unaware of sexual abuse, let alone its prolificacy or the compulsion of its perpetrators. No one was to know this secret crime. I just had a visceral feeling that Cadman was bad for children.

I was not the only one. The chaplain, John Presswell, resigned after a short while and wrote to AMMA (the Assistant Masters and Mistresses Association) on 13 September 1981:

> Now that I have left the School, it all seems like an incredible dream or even a nightmare. Perhaps the biggest single factor that springs to mind immediately and for which the Principal was directly responsible was the deep unhappiness and intense frustration that so many of

> the boys experienced continually. I would almost regard it as criminal when they were subjected to further and totally unnecessary frustration which often reduced them to tears or at least panic about their future. Boys pleaded not to go to Maths lessons taught by Mr. Cadman, not only because they did not learn anything, there was such inability to control the class, but because when he did suddenly attempt to enforce his control through various punishments, these were meted out at random, excessively and generally to the wrong boys. When the boys were talking to me, they often revealed that they had knowledge of facts which I knew to be confidential. The source of such information always led back to the indiscretion of the Principal, either in what he said to a boy or what he had left lying around his room to which many boys had authorized and unauthorized access. One clear incident was when a number of boys became inebriated in school. It was discovered that they had obtained the alcohol from the Principal's flat. On bringing the matter to the Principal with the evidence, he not only refused to take any disciplinary action, but denied that the boys had done it. I also recall a visit to Reading by a number of older boys where they met the Principal in a public house and came back in a distinctly unsteady state.

It was all undesirable, unprofessional, and unacceptable. In the absence of any other answer, I thought it would be wise to open up the question to "the authorities" first of all in the person of our elected representative, Sir Michael McNair-Wilson, MP for Newbury. "The authorities" must be wiser than me. It never occurred to me that they were not. I made an appointment for a small group of teachers to see him in his room at the House of Commons in April 1981. He ushered us into a committee room. Rays of spring sunshine lit up its wooden panelling. We knew that this was the start of something. The MP pulled out a small piece of paper from his inside pocket. We drew breath. Half an hour later, the paper covered with scratchings, he had given up taking notes, his eyes were fixed on us as we presented him with a stream of events which, taken out of context were simply ludicrous, but showed a world full of children in which Cadman was a manic God dispensing edicts, exercising summary judgments, making his minions appear and disappear—all-powerful, utterly wilful, and quite out-of-control.

What would "the authorities" do? The answer was twofold. Very little and they made it worse.

What I did not realise until I interviewed Esther Rantzen decades later (7 April 2015) was that the MP thought it was all motivated by professional jealousy. "Staff versus staff. He distanced himself from it," Esther told me while I was writing this book. Indeed, his last letter to me after her broadcasts affirmed the obvious (dated 8 March 1989): "In this country, a person is innocent until proved guilty, so I do not think I should comment further on the matter." In the local press (*Newbury Weekly News*, 29 June 1989), he accepted that constituents had expressed concerns, but stated that no one had introduced a sexual element. I thought at the time that we were being let down by the authorities and thirty-four years later I knew that this was absolutely correct. "A sexual element". That was what was lacking. The other aspects of neglect and abuse counted for little compared to this. It seems this is still true. Matthew Grey's electrocution was not taken further by the police. That devastating torment had been inflicted on him via his nipples was not considered abusive enough. His underpants remained in situ; his penis was unexposed, untouched. Had it been, I was told, this would have made the difference.

Back in 1981, I was heartened that Michael McNair-Wilson reported the thrust of our meeting to Dr. Rhodes Boyson, the then secretary of state for education. Rhodes Boyson wrote to him on 1 June 1981:

Thank you for your letter expressing concern about Crookham Court School, Newbury.

The Secretary of State's powers in relation to independent schools are set out in sections 70–76 of the Education Act 1944. Independent schools must register with the Department and certain minimum standards are expected of them in respect of premises, accommodation, quality of tuition and staffing. If a school is seriously deficient in one or more of these areas and has failed to make the necessary improvements after a reasonable time a Notice of Complaint may be served. This requires the matters complained of to be remedied within six months failing which, subject to an appeal to an Independent Schools Tribunal, the Secretary of State may delete the name of the school from the register of independent schools, effectively requiring it to close. This action may also be taken if the proprietor is considered to be "not a proper person to be proprietor of an independent school", though there would, of course, have to be firm evidence to substantiate such a charge. The issuing of a Notice of Complaint is a serious step and it is regarded as a last resort where other measures have failed or are considered inappropriate.

Independent schools are subject to inspection by HM Inspectorate of Schools in the same way as maintained schools and it so happens that the HM Inspector who is responsible for liaising with Crookham Court School is visiting the school this term.

The Department will consider the matter further in the light of HM Inspector's report and I will write to you again then.

The inspector and his colleague visited Cadman in June 1981. They told him that a group of his staff had complained about him to an MP.

Cadman reacted with fury, summoning the staff to a meeting on 9 June 1981 during which he told the staff he had received twenty-two replies to his advertisement for posts. Such posts at a boys' boarding school in the country were popular, especially when little by way of a reference was required.

He demanded the names of those who had been to the MP. When he received no answer, he listed his demands, as the minutes of the meeting record:

1. What are the nature of your complaints?
2. When did you complain?
3. To whom did you complain?
4. Were you present at the meeting at The Paddocks at the end of last term?
5. Why did you not keep the Headmaster informed?
6. Why did you not advise me of your action?
7. What did you hope to gain by your action?
8. Do you wish to remain at Crookham Court in view of your action?
9. Who signed the document?
10. How did you get the information?
11. Have you any other complaints and if so would you read them out?

The minutes also record: "A lengthy silence followed. All members of staff remained silent."

The inspectors arrived a few weeks later. In 1981 their reports were secret. Not even the MP was supposed to see their findings. He did, however, and sent me a copy. It was not flattering. Extracts follow from the *Report by HM Inspectors on Crookham Court Independent School inspected 30 November—2 December 1981'*:

> Although it is not uncommon in small independent schools to find that a regular capitation allowance is not made to

departments, it is certainly unusual to find, as here, that the headmaster has no funds, not even petty cash, available to enable educational policy to be reinforced.

... The standard of work by pupils, as seen in lessons and by examining their exercise books varies from subject to subject and teacher to teacher, but overall it must be categorised as poor. In a number of subjects, teachers are able to interest the boys who then work well to produce creditable responses. In too many cases, however, the pupils' lack of motivation is not overcome, their interest is dampened rather than fired and the consequence is poor involvement and output.

... A tuck shop is run by one of the senior boys who keeps the profits he makes. This does not seem an appropriate way of organising the tuck shop; profits could more reasonably be devoted to a fund used to improve the facilities for all pupils.

... The school is managed as a limited company with the proprietor as chairman and one other director. The proprietor also acts as principal and has sole responsibility for financial and domestic arrangements including the appointment and dismissal of all staff. The final decision on any matter, educational or other, rests with him. As stated by the proprietor, a headmaster is appointed "to ensure the daily running of the school", but he has very limited powers.

... Of the 103 boys who have left since 1978, 42 have stayed only one year or less and a further 35 have stayed between one and two years. Just 24 have stayed more than three years of whom only nine remained the full five years.

One wonders why nine stayed so long.

I took one of the inspectors aside and said, "Cadman is just appalling and the place is falling apart. We wanted you to come and see for yourselves how rotten everything is. It needs to be shut down."

The Inspector looked me straight in the eye and said, "If it's not worse than the worst inner-city state school, there's nothing we can do."

And nothing was exactly what happened. The school remained as run-down as ever, none of the inspectors' recommendations was addressed, and when another inspection occurred in 1988, all that happened was that the failings were restated. By that time, however, the inspection reports were published and the conclusions hit the press.

"Officials condemn 'dirty, dispiriting' boarding school" read *The Daily Telegraph* headline on 27 October 1988. "When inspectors visited Crookham Court, near Newbury, Berks, last November, they found 33 safety hazards, ranging from broken glass in the shrubbery to live wires protruding from a dormitory wall."

In 1981, no one knew. Here are some extracts from the 1981 Report. In the seven years between then and 1988, nothing had changed.

> The gymnasium is still inadequate and is full of hazards [page 3]; ... washbasins and WCs are outside in an unheated block adapted from part of a garage [page 3]; it is undesirable that ten and eleven year olds should be required to walk in dressing gowns through the grounds to the main building for their baths, especially on cold dark nights.
>
> ... throughout the school needs surveying. There are loose wires, broken switches, empty lamp sockets, patched-up flex to electric fires. Many electric lamps and their fittings were broken at the time of the inspection. All of these could present a safety risk and require urgent attention [page 4]; [in the gymnasium] slivers of glass were found on the floor, equipment was worn or

> unstable. This unhygienic and possibly dangerous state of affairs is unsatisfactory and should not be allowed to continue [page 24].

The inspectors concluded, "General standards of cleanliness and maintenance need to be improved and hazards to health and safety need to be eliminated." Absolutely nothing was done.

"Not a fit and proper person": I could not see how Cadman could be seen as anything other than neither "fit" nor "proper". The fine words were useless. I sent Sir Michael letter after letter. He told me he would write to the new education secretary, Sir Keith Joseph. Sir Keith's letter to Sir Michael was utterly clear. Basically, if a school was bad, parents wouldn't send their children to it and it would close. In his words (letter to Sir Michael McNair-Wilson dated 25 July 1983):

> If I am satisfied that an independent school is "objectionable" by virtue of either its unsatisfactory tuition and accommodation or the proprietor's (or any teacher's) not being a "proper person", I serve a notice of complaint against the school. Subject to a right of appeal of the Independent Schools Tribunal, the school can be struck from the Register if the matters complained of are not rectified. This makes its continued operation a criminal offence.
>
> I remain of the view, though, that market forces can exert powerful pressure on standards. Mr. Mucklejohn and I will have to agree to differ on the efficacy of such forces. I concede that they may not always work either speedily or in apparently the most efficient direction. It may be, of course, that the fault in such cases is not in the action of the market forces themselves, but our expectation of what those forces should achieve.

My arguments—that market forces could not apply when the person receiving the service had to receive the service by law, was not paying for it himself, and tended as he was underage not to be believed anyway, carried no weight. Crookham Court, in spite of inspectors' caveats strong enough to make headline news when they were repeated five years later, was not "objectionable".

As much of the "market" for Crookham Court places came from service families and the fees were paid from public money, I tried, via Sir Michael, the Ministry of Defence. Crookham Court appeared on the list of schools for which the services allowance was paid. I suggested it should not be so approved. In a letter to Sir Michael dated 6 June 1983, the junior armed forces minister Jerry Wiggin wrote: "In order that servicemen might qualify for receipt of the allowance, all schools used by their children must be fully registered with the Department of Education and Science. The choice of school is a matter solely for the parents."

The Ministry of Defence did not seem to find the school "objectionable" either.

In light of the media publicity given to the school in 1988 following another negative inspection, I again tackled Sir Michael on this (letter dated 1 November 1988):

> The interesting point is that, as "The Telegraph" says (article October 27 1988), "This school caters mainly ... for Service families who choose to have their children educated at the taxpayer's expense." Unless the situation has changed in the last five years, it seems that a school can be kept afloat on taxpayer's money, provided the school is "fully registered" with the DES. I do not know, incidentally, how a school can be other than "fully registered". I do not think it can be "partly registered". In any case, we can see how unsatisfactory a school can be—and still receive public money.

When children are in a school, [the Ministry of Defence] is generally unwilling to allow them to change as one reason for placing them in boarding education in the first place is to provide continuity—however unsuitable that continuity may be, it would appear.

I wonder if the rules need looking at again in the light of this nonsensical situation to see if a list of specifically recommended schools would be more appropriate. As it is, the "market forces" Sir Keith Joseph mentioned in his last letter have been positive ones created by taxpayers' money.

And how about the BBC? In the early 1980s, the investigative radio programme *Checkpoint* exposed St George's School in Stowmarket. A teacher was reportedly dismissed for talking to a social worker. There were "reigns of terror". All kinds of improper behaviour were occurring. The pattern was a familiar one. I wrote to the programme (letter 13 September 1982):

What you have done is to highlight a situation which has become possible in independent schools following the Government's withdrawal of the status of "recognized as efficient" in 1978. It is now entirely possible for almost anyone who wants to buy a school and run it almost as he wishes. In cases where parents are far away, the proprietor of such a school is accountable only to himself and it gives such a proprietor the possibility for more power over people than can obtain in any other business—children sent to these schools must be educated by law; they cannot walk out; they have to accept what comes their way.

A proprietor can be completely unsuitable to run a school. He can have been dismissed for incompetence from other schools; he can be unstable; he can be disturbed. He can still have power over children. Parents who suspect something is wrong will remove their children—if they are close enough to the school to keep contact with it. Staff who disapprove will leave—but teaching jobs are hard to come by. The parents of boarders are often overseas and so remain in ignorance and tend to disbelieve children's stories anyway. Local Education Authorities are only too happy to find a private school willing to take children—particularly disturbed children—in their care and do not ask too many questions. Staff who are afraid of unemployment tolerate the situation and to keep their jobs may have to perpetuate it by presenting a facade of normality.

Before 1978, a school had to undergo rigorous inspection by Her Majesty's Inspectors before it was "recognized". If there were anything wrong with the proprietor, the school would not be recognized. This system was dropped in 1978 as it was considered anomalous by the then Government to spend public money on HMIs inspecting and approving private schools. Not all children who attend public school are financed privately, though. A considerable number are paid for out of public funds—by the Ministry of Defence and Local Education Authorities, for example. Yet these children and these funds can go to proprietors who have never been inspected for recognition and may be incompetent or undesirable. They have simply started or taken over private schools since the mid-1970s. There are schools advertised for sale from time to time. All that is needed is the money to buy the school and the staff are paid to do as they are told.

It is not particularly difficult to recruit pupils either. The "Educational Trusts" rarely visit the schools they "recommend" and can be unaware that a school has changed hands. A "recommendation" from such a prestigious body carries some weight with parents. The "guardians" of some foreign children in this country can have commission arrangements with schools if they recommend their "wards" to them. Even if a school does not make a profit, it can be used as a tax loss. It can give someone with the money to buy a school the chance to put into practice his own ideas of how to educate children—however bizarre these ideas may be.

If teachers have fears about a proprietor to the extent that they believe he is affecting the normal development of children, what can they do? The Union will be sympathetic, advise seeking employment elsewhere and point out the difficulty of getting anything done. An M. P. will express concern and disbelief that the system can permit such abuses of power. Even if an Inspectors' visit results, classroom teaching and facilities will be looked at. The Inspectors will not encourage the reporting to them of incidents or even of concern. The Inspectors' report will be confidential to the school and the proprietor need not reveal any of its contents to the staff. Recommendations may be made, cosmetic changes may result, but the fundamental problem—the unsuitability of the proprietor to be in charge of children—will remain. The onus is now on others to prove by hard evidence the unsuitability of a proprietor of an independent school, not for that proprietor to prove his suitability at an inspection. Staff risk reprisals and ultimately their jobs for very little indeed.

It was suggested by the Editor of "The Good Schools Guide" that the case in question is an isolated one. I know it is not. All the above has happened at another school.

The response I had from the producer, John Edwards (letter, 17 September 1982) thanked me for my letter "and the helpful comments it contained". Nothing else. How about the Independent Schools Association Incorporated? Crookham Court was a member. I wrote (letter 14 June 1983):

> I understand that for Membership of your Association certain standards pertain. I should be grateful if you could advise me what checks are made on the suitability of proprietors—in particular sole proprietors of your Member schools to hold such positions.
>
> I am told that a local independent school, Crookham Court School, is a Member of your Association. I should greatly appreciate knowing if you have recently re-assessed this establishment for continuing Membership following its change of ownership in 1977 and its changes of Headmaster in 1977, 1978 and 1982 and, if so, to know if this School still satisfies your "Qualifications for Membership".

There was no response.

What about advice from the Independent Schools Information Service (ISIS)? It, too, listed Crookham Court. My letter to them (on 12 May 1981) read:

> At present ISIS provides information on and seemingly gives reassurance to parents on the suitability of independent schools for their children. There is, however, no system of inspection or standards required to justify recommendation of any particular school.
>
> The knowledge that we have of a most disquieting situation in an independent school, jeopardising the integrity of independent schooling in general and our belief in ISIS in particular cannot be acted on because there is no provision for inspection, assessment or accountability.
>
> While supporting freedom of choice, I believe that this should be an informed choice. The "information" explicit in ISIS's title should imply objectivity, not just "advertisement".

Crookham Court continued in membership of both bodies.

Nothing from the Ministry; nothing from the BBC; nothing from august bodies furthering the aims of private schools. I sensed that officialdom was annoyed by my persistence. Many of them had been through private school. I seemed to be intruding on a private world that flourished best in shade. The glare of publicity had finished off St George's. Seven years on it was to finish off Crookham Court, but not yet. A few more years had to pass and a few more lives had to be devastated before the horror of it all was to hit the nation's TV screens.

All these organisations seemed to exist to protect people, to offer assurance. In fact, all they did was give credibility to a system that allowed anyone to have access to children with complete impunity. Had there been a necessity for Cadman to prove his suitability to be in charge of children, he would not have been able to do this. He was never questioned about his background. Because he was rich enough, he could buy his own school and buy everyone in it. In addition, public money was being used to provide him with a supply of potential victims.

But I had missed a clue. I had even written it down. In a letter on 19 March 1983, I wrote to Michael McNair-Wilson: "We discussed briefly the issues arising from Roger Cook's 'Checkpoint' programme on St. George's School, Stowmarket—where the majority of the boys come from Army families. Although the HMI's report on this school did not support the points raised in the programme, the BBC, I gather, still maintains that they are true. I read in 'The Times' that the Headmaster, Mr. Slade has resigned. He visited Crookham Court some days ago and I understand that Crookham Court is now hoping to attract boys from Army families by offering a discount on fees. I assume a connection has been established."

"A connection". It was a word I used in all innocence, unaware of its ramifications. In the fullness of time Derek Slade was imprisoned for twenty-one years for child sex abuse. It was paedophile meeting paedophile. It was as if they knew where they could strike with impunity. Of course, they did.

At that time I had simply no idea how relevant my copy letter was.

Even in my ignorance, my letter (21 May 1983) to Michael McNair-Wilson after Sir Keith's was prophetic:

> The point that concerns us both, I think, in the light of our discussions and also the "Checkpoint" revelations, is that an independent school can become the domain of a single person in which this person has more power over others than is possible in any other "normal" situation. There must be provision in the Education Act to prevent unsuitable people having this power. There must, therefore, be some definition of suitability. At present, we know that anyone can be in this position after being dismissed from other schools, being incompetent, being ill, or can use his position to act out fantasies or eccentricities. It is unusual; it is bizarre, but it does happen—and not only in Newbury. There must be an introduction of requirements for suitability to run private schools within the meaning of the Education Act which will prevent abuses. Those existing are insufficient.
>
> "Market forces" often take a long time to have any effect and sometimes, surprisingly, apply far less than might be thought. The problem is that the "market" (the person paying for the service) is not the one who receives it (the school pupil). It is anomalous that the recipient of the service must—by law—receive this service and yet has—by law—little protection from it. Parents are often in ignorance of what happens in boarding schools—especially if they are at a distance which is, of course, one of the main reasons for opting for a private boarding education in the first place.
>
> "Market forces" will not do much to prevent an eccentric prepared to pay for the privilege from abusing the autonomy a private boarding school situation provides.

> Staff will remain silent for fear of unemployment; pupils will not be believed; HMI's reports will be guardedly phrased. We know there is little that can, at present, be done. Private schools are very closed communities.
>
> The independent sector's own "accreditation arrangements" are quite inadequate and are based on the assumption that schools are run by decent, well-intentioned people. ISIS does not analyse proprietors' backgrounds, or judge their suitability. This seems to be taken for granted. Membership of such a body suggests the attainment of some sort of standard, but this is illusory. From the "Qualifications for Membership" of the Independent Schools Association, it is clear that it, like other bodies, has only vague ideals.
>
> What can be done? What other scandals have to emerge?

The answer, of course, was sex.

EIGHT

Telling—and hiding—the truth

Until 1983, I had no idea what child sex abuse was. It had never entered my life. When it did, I assumed that all abused children told a trusted adult and that the trusted adult told the authorities and the authorities took action. It seemed so logical. And that's what happened—at least the first part. The abused child told a trusted adult—me. After this point, the logic broke down and there was nothing I could do about it. I suddenly became complicit in a cover-up.

It was at this point that I should have realised there was more to the nonsense than a crazy old man whose views wouldn't be given the time of day in any other place, standing on top of a pile of rubble, human frailty, and failed ambitions, and giving his existence some meaning.

(Personal conversation, May 1983): Tom, a prefect, came into my classroom after lunch. "Sir," he said, "Malcolm [not his real name] … asked me if I would ask you if he could speak to you."

"Why didn't he come himself?"

"Don't know. He's upset about something."

"OK. Tell him to come at break. Here."

Malcolm came at break. He was a bright boy, chirpy and responsive, thirteen years-old. This was not the same child.

His face was grim, set, aged. I knew this was not going to be a general chat about his prep. "This is something serious, isn't it?"

"Yes."

I sensed what was to come.

"It involves a teacher, doesn't it?"

"Yes."

"OK. You'll have to use your own words. I can't put words into your mouth."

The tears came. His face went through white to red.

"It was last night. I was in bed. Everyone was asleep. I woke up. I felt something in my bed. A hand was in the bed. It went into my pyjamas. It pulled them open and …" Malcolm's eyes raced as he fought for the word. "I don't know the word."

"I think you know the word you use. Don't worry. Just go on."

This little boy sat in front of me in the most surreal encounter of my life. All the trappings of the classroom were there. The posters were on the wall; the books on the shelves, the graffiti on the desk; the previous lesson on the blackboard. I was "Sir"; he was the pupil. He was using the language of the playground to describe the most intimate details of his body, not jokingly to a friend, but in the full knowledge that what he was going to say would have consequences beyond the immediate and, of all things, to a teacher. The inappropriateness of the swear words, the incongruity of the situation, it all came down on him. The only tissue I had was paper for cleaning the board. It was hard and green. I gave it to Malcolm. Eyes, nose, mouth, all were running. I ached to stop it all. It was coming and I didn't want to hear it. I wanted to push it back, stop him telling it. I wanted to tell it for him, to put it into sanitised language, dispassionate, cold, clinical, to remove it from him like a surgical operation, to detach it from what was personal, to hold it up and analyse it like a piece of literary criticism. To kill it and dissect it. Not to have it coming as it was, crude, hot, moist as the mucus from his nose. He shook. It was coming and I couldn't stop it.

"Go on." I sounded detached and hoped it would pass on to Malcolm.

"It was Mr. Hoade [not his real name], Sir. He was at the side of my bed. His hand went on my prick."

"Yes."

"And then he moved it up and down. He wanked me. It went on and on."

"Didn't you cry out? Didn't you yell?"

"No. I couldn't. It hurt. He …"

"Who's 'he'?"

"Mr. Hoade."

"Go on."

"He pulled my prick. He wanked me. I didn't know what to do."

"How long did it last?"

"Don't know."

"Then what?"

"He went out."

"Did he say anything to you?"

"No."

"What did you do?"

"I just lay there and then I saw Tom this morning and asked if he would see you."

I felt I couldn't offer sympathy. He was making an allegation. It would result in dismissal, parents laying charges, a court case. I was merely the instrument for its revelation. The human part of me that went out to this little boy who had revealed all that was innermost had to be subdued. I had absolutely no doubt that what he had told me was true. Never had I seen such emotion; never had I been closer to the soul.

"What you have told me is very serious. You know that? You need to tell it to the headmaster, too. Stay here and I'll get him."

I ran to the study. The then head was Gordon Gooding. He was a man in his forties. Blond, slight, awkward. I asked

Malcolm to tell again what he had told me. He did. He was calmer now. The sobs came more slowly.

Gooding was able to detach himself far better than me. Malcolm's prick became an object for analysis. Gooding used the medical term and asked Malcolm if Mr. Hoade had pulled his penis; to what extent he had pulled his penis; how far the foreskin had been lowered. "Do you normally have difficulty retracting your foreskin?" Malcolm had no idea what he was getting at. Neither had I. He answered as best he could. Malcolm had been touched. He had been invaded. That was enough. Malcolm's penis assumed enormous proportions as an entity on its own. It was almost funny. This little boy sitting discussing the extent of his penile flexibility with two grown men and all the time the only point at issue was, "He wanked me, Sir."

From that moment not another word was said to me about Malcolm's allegation. I asked Gooding if he had told Cadman. He told me he had and that he was leaving it to Cadman to decide what to do. It took two days. Rumours were rife. Word had got out that Malcolm had been touched by Hoade. Christopher Hoade was a master popular with several boys. He was hospitable. He lived in "The Paddocks", a house that had been the chaplain's, now converted into dorms and masters' bedsits. Hoade stopped teaching. Gooding told me that was at Cadman's request.

Hoade was never dismissed. He left quietly several days later and made an appearance at Speech and Sports Day a few months after that, invited by Cadman. Malcolm's parents were never told. I begged Gooding to tell them. "Up to Mr. Cadman," was the response. No point in talking to Cadman. I tried my solicitor. "Here is a boy who has been sexually assaulted and his parents don't know. Someone has to tell them. What would your advice be if I told you I wanted to tell them?"

"Don't do it. He could bring a case against you for damaging his business."

I left it at that. In the year or two that followed, Malcolm became a difficult boy. He was punished for mooning when he was in the minibus. We never again spoke about what had happened. I asked his brother if Malcolm had spoken to his parents and suggested that maybe he should do so. That's as far as I went.

I assumed that all sexually assaulted schoolboys sought the counsel of a sympathetic teacher the next day. How wrong I was. And even then I failed to realise that what was happening was the tip of the iceberg; a paedophile was recruiting paedophiles. A paedophile was not disclosing the behaviour of other paedophiles. I had tacitly let a crime go unpunished; a child victim left uncounselled. I feared an expensive lawsuit and, in effect, let the paedophile buy my silence. They can.

Staff with tastes in other directions found that they could avail themselves freely of the boys. During a meeting of all the local English teachers, taking advantage of Crookham's spacious library and on-tap catering services to mark the CSE papers, a visiting teacher decided to find one of her former pupils, now an assistant matron. With Norman Wishaw (not his real name), another English teacher, I wrote a memo to Cadman.

> To SPC and AJG.
>
> An embarrassing incident has occurred which we must report to you.
>
> At the CSE Moderation this evening, one of the visiting teachers went into the kitchen and told us she had discovered a boy—Gideon Farmer [not his real name]—kissing one of the kitchen staff. The lady in question had a cigarette in her hand. Miss D was also in the kitchen at the time.
>
> IGM & NW 19 May 1983

Inappropriate behaviour for staff? Shouldn't be smoking in the kitchen? Must rescue the boy from the clutches of predatory females. Voyeurism among the vol-au-vents. Not a bit of it. We were roundly rebuked (letter, 15 June 1983):

> There are certain aspects of the case which have not been elaborated very fully and which I now outline; about which I would like further information.
>
> 1. Was it a continental kiss, i.e. a peck on both cheeks, or something more meaningful?
> 2. Were the participants standing, sitting or lying down?
> 3. The lady in question had a cigarette in one hand. Please describe the situation more precisely.
> 4. What was the duration of the incident?
> 5. What was the visiting teacher herself doing in the kitchen?
> 6. Permission is given to use the Library. On no account should visitors be permitted to wander around into the kitchen without authority. Will you please give me your assurance that this will not happen again.
>
> Yours sincerely,
>
> S. P. Cadman

There we were. It was all our fault that the visitor had been embarrassed. She should not have been there. The reply was passed round the visitor's school and all the other schools in West Berkshire and beyond. It caused much laughter. The incident was not mentioned again.

The boy was, though.

NINE

Gideon's story

Gideon was an interesting boy. He came to Crookham Court at about the age of twelve. Handsome, blond hair, large eyes, and dark eyebrows. He was quite a favourite. Like many of the boys, he was from an army background. He was not a reader or writer, but he was quick on the uptake and saw various opportunities. One of these was to build the school minibus. One might imagine that this would be best entrusted to a garage or a specialist firm. Not at all. Gideon bought a Transit van with Cadman's money, cut squares for the windows, screwed in seats and belts and that was that. A van became a minibus.

His special status with Cadman did not go unnoticed. The staff meeting minutes of 6 July 1983 give a hint of the mood prevailing.

> Matters arising. Mr. Mucklejohn noted that Gideon Farmer had been mentioned at the previous Meeting and enquired as to the current situation regarding this boy, because he was not attending his normal classes, a matter which he had reported to the Headmaster.
>
> Mr. Gooding replied that as Gideon was not prepared to obey his authority and submit to the normal discipline

of the School, he had placed himself outside the control of the School and this he (Mr. Gooding) had reported to Mr. Cadman. Mr. Gooding said that, in the circumstances, he could not see how he could be responsible for Gideon Farmer and he did not expect staff to be either, but that Mr. Mucklejohn was correct to report his absence and thanked him for so doing. He added that Gideon Farmer had been relieved of his duties as a sub-prefect but still enjoyed the title.

Mr. Wishaw asked if Mr. Cadman would make a statement relevant to the position of Gideon Farmer in the School. Mr. Cadman replied that in recent days he had permission to work on the minibus and that some work had been effected on it which he was about to inspect.

Mr. Wishaw, supported by other members of staff, pointed out that Gideon was spending up to two hours on the telephone at a time. Mr. Cadman replied that he should be stopped and that all boys should only be allowed a maximum of five minutes on the telephone. Concern was then expressed as to the means of getting Gideon to obey instructions.

Mr. Gooding added that the boy had refused on more than one occasion to obey his authority and that this had been reported to the Principal. On the last occasion, Gideon Farmer had in his presence also refused to obey Mr. Cadman and on that occasion had also sworn in the presence of the Principal and Headmaster. Mr. Cadman interjected that when he ripped out the telephone wires, Gideon then ceased using the telephone. Mr. Gooding agreed, but pointed out that Gideon had then stormed off swearing and indicating that he would now have to go outside to use a public call box and that he had not obeyed Mr. Cadman's instructions to go to his lessons.

Mr. Cadman said that prefects should be used to make Gideon Farmer do as he was told. The staff and

> Headmaster protested that this would involve the use of physical force or the threat of physical force which was not the appropriate action for professional teachers. As Mr. Cadman did not agree with this point, he was asked to explain in more detail how the prefects could be involved. Mr. Cadman refused to discuss the issue any further. Mr. Gooding closed the discussion by reporting to Mr. Cadman that Gideon Farmer had refused to acknowledge his authority and to obey reasonable instructions from him. Under these circumstances, he had to report the boy beyond the control of himself and his staff.

Gideon was being thoroughly cultivated. He remained faithful to Cadman to the end. As a young man he came back to the school in 1989 when it was besieged by reporters and TV cameras, even going so far as to drive his BMW at one of them, the dust cloud captured on film in perpetuity.

Before he came to Crookham, Gideon told me, he had spent much of his time at Diana Dors's home with his friend, her son. He loved the family and remembered them with affection. While he was telling me this I felt then, as I did years afterwards, that there was something more to say; something to get across. One summer afternoon in 1983, I found him standing in my classroom at break.

"Is there something, Gideon?"

He nodded.

"Well, I have to rush now, but can you make it another time?"

Another nod.

The opportunity never returned. After leaving school, before the scandal broke, he would come to my home occasionally. He arrived, invariably in a black leather jacket and driving a smart black sports saloon. He would come into my study and sit in silence. I broke it with inconsequential conversation. Whatever it was he had come to say—and come to say something he clearly had—he never did.

Thirty years passed before I found out what had been on his mind and what, thirty years later, still was. Again it was Facebook that renewed the acquaintance. I was surprised to receive a friend request from him. We chatted online (Facebook, 16 August 2014): "Cadman opened up to me and told me his story he didnt try anything with me but as you know i had that hold on him and could do what i wanted."

"So why would Cadman open up to you?"

"who knows but i think he would let me get aways with things and even when i was found out i wouldnt drop him in it and he then trusted me. I think he trusted me after i was driving the minbus to take him somewhere and was reported to the police and didnt say a thing about him and just said i had the keys and waned to take it for a drive."

"He made you complicit. All this was a big secret for a young boy to keep. Was it that that you were going to tell me that summer's day all those years ago?"

"it could well have been."

"Oh, Gideon, how I wish you had. That would have been the key. It all seems so obvious now, but we never suspected that at the time. So many young lives have been affected by that man and all that he let happen. It must have been a big burden to carry."

"it has followed me i have done the same things dont say a thing and use it and get what i can out of it and walk over anyone who gets in my way that has been my life from the age 13 to date."

"Come and see me. It's been a while."

(Personal meeting at my home, 30 September 2014): After a gap of thirty years, Gideon again came down my drive, walking this time. The years had been kind to him. He was tall, dark-haired now with a hint of grey. His eyes moved quickly, taking in his surroundings.

"They've dropped me off," he told me. "They'll come when I call them. They won't be far away."

"Friends?"

Gideon looked at me as if I should know better. "They work for me."

Friends were not part of Gideon's mindset and had not been from an early age. His parents had been in the forces and he had lived mainly with his nan. When he was old enough, he had been sent to a boarding prep school. He described it without affection. "I never wanted to go to lessons there. They didn't know what to do with me. They tried to get me into doing things I wanted to do like making a set for the stage. I liked that, but when they tried to get me to go into lessons, I didn't want to and refused, so they punished me. I told them it wouldn't work, punishing me. If they gave me the cane or the slipper, I told them it would be bad for them. I'd do things like loosen the valves on the radiator so it flooded the rooms below. I just turned whatever they wanted to do to me into something that was bad for them.

"They sent me off to do jobs like sweeping up in the little church down the road. I met all sorts of people there, the sorts that have been put on community service and that kind of thing. One of them said to me, 'Blow all this, I'll burn the bloody place down tonight. Won't have to sweep it out.' And he did. He burnt it down that night. So I didn't have to sweep it out either."

That had been Gideon's way ever since he could remember. Self-preservation. Using his knowledge to save a church from destruction had not occurred to him. "I'd have had to sweep it." Incurring the displeasure of teachers was irrelevant. "They couldn't do anything for me." Pleasing people was not in his mind. "If they can do something for me, like a bank, I'll be nice to them; tell them what they want to hear. They think I'm well-spoken and I know how to dress. If not …" he spread his arms and gave a slight shrug to the shoulders as if the answer were obvious. To him, it was. Relating to people was not his forte. I felt privileged that he should come and see me. Of all the people he knew I was probably the only one who understood why he was as he was. "No one can work me out," he said. "Oh, I can," I replied.

At his prep school he was in the same class as Diana Dors's son. "We hit it off and he said to me one half-term, why not come and stay with me? So I did and she said come back whenever you have a holiday, so I did. She had to become my guardian for this to be allowed and so she was responsible for me all the time I was at that school. I spent a lot of time living in her house. She was kind, but she had to turn on her acting side, though, and there were lots of parties. We were locked in our room while they were on, but I knew how these celebrities behaved. Her husband was a drunk and the place was full of things to do with drugs. At other times, we shot around the garden on little motor bikes. When we were out with her, she was recognised wherever she went and people used to feed us ice creams and pay us a lot of attention. I never wanted for anything.

"When prep school came to an end, I went to Crookham. I suppose it was because it was on the forces' list and the fees matched the forces' grant. I was just the same there. I didn't want to go to lessons and I didn't have to. Cadman let me do what I wanted to do. I just became his driver."

"How did you get into that position? Did he try anything on with you?"

"He made a move once and I pushed him away. He never tried it again. I could do what I wanted. I knew what he was and he knew I knew it. He just gave me whatever I asked for. Once I told him he should buy a new car, so I told him to give me a cheque for a new Simca Ranchero."

"I'd often wondered how he came to choose a Simca Ranchero. It's an odd choice for a man approaching seventy."

"He'd do what I told him to do. I took the cheque, paid for the car and pocketed the cashback they were offering on it.

That's why it was a Ranchero. Same with the minibus. I took a cheque for the minibus, bought a Transit van instead and converted it into a minibus. Drove it, too, when I was fifteen. Had a load of boys in it.

"Whatever I wanted, he'd get it for me. I had the run of the school. I used to go wherever I wanted. I knew what was happening, but it didn't bother me. I knew there were boys in his room. That's why he bought the school. Had to borrow money off his relatives to do this and pay them back for years. He wanted to be where there were boys. Didn't want to run a school, though.

"He wanted to know what other people were doing. There were boys all over the place in his flat. I thought everyone knew what was happening. I used to go to The Paddocks where Hoade lived. He used to talk all the time about what he did with boys. The boys were there while he was talking about it. Cadman wanted to know what he was doing and which boys he was with. I used to drive Hoade and Cadman to the gay pub in Newbury in his Land-Rover. I was about fifteen. They'd put me in an upstairs room while I was waiting for them. Only got caught by the police once and I never dropped Cadman in it. I said I'd found the keys and took it for a spin. Then I asked him to get me a car and he did. I took him everywhere. All around London. He knew all the places gay people went to.

"There were lots of people around—in his room at the school, at his flat in London. Met his relatives, too. They were pretty eccentric."

"But there must have come a time when you left school."

"I don't think I was ever there. Never went to lessons. Ran the tuck shop. Made money. I had a caravan there eventually."

He had no interest in what his peers thought of him. They were his customers. They would give him money. That was his interest.

"How about the headmasters?"

"Freeman was OK, but Gooding tried to stop me doing what I wanted and he had to go."

"So you're the one who wrote him the note with letters cut from newspapers—'The Good times are over'?"

"Yes." Gideon smiled at the recollection. "He was getting in my way. That's what happens to people who get in my way. He went."

All this was Gideon's normality. "It's what I do in business," he said. "I've never known anything else. If it's a situation I can use for my benefit, I will."

"You were taking the principal of a school, your school, around gay bars at the age of fifteen with teachers. You knew there were boys in his room. You knew Hoade was intimate with boys in his room."

"Yes. And I knew boys were with the kitchen staff. I knew all this. He knew I wouldn't say anything and I got whatever I wanted."

"And it never occurred to you that all this was wrong? Incredibly wrong? Morally wrong?"

"It was OK for me. I was getting what I wanted. If I get what I want, it's OK. I used to live there in the holidays, too."

"Didn't your parents wonder where you were?"

"Hardly ever saw them. In fact, I got to know my dad only in the last two years of his life when he retired to Cornwall. There he was doing half marathons, living a healthy life and he died at sixty-two. Just like that."

"Have you always been amoral?"

"If there's nothing in it for me, I'm not interested."

"You were there at the end when Gold was headmaster. You must've been nineteen, so you weren't still at the school, were you?"

"I used to do things for Cadman. He asked me to help him when he was arrested. 'You'll go to jail,' I told him. 'No,' he said. 'You'll go to jail. I know what'll happen.' Then he asked me to destroy all the papers. I hired a van and took them in loads and burnt them. He didn't want the police contacting people who'd been at the school. In those days, it wasn't so easy to find people. He wanted everything destroyed and he paid me. It must've been £20–25,000, something like that. Gold's car got in the way of my van. I smashed it up.

"It's all about money and getting it. If I'm building a house and I need a staircase that costs £20,000, I'll do business that's worth £20,000 and buy it."

Gideon visited Cadman in the 1990s after his release from prison, but there was nothing in it for him and he stopped visiting. It must have been on those occasions that he also visited me and said nothing. Now he was content to talk.

"You have children. What values do you want them to have?"

"I can tell them what'll happen if they do something, so they shouldn't do it."

"But what example are you to them?"

I doubted if Gideon had been asked that question before. His children were brought up by their mothers, he told me. He shrugged his shoulders.

"And your girlfriend now? The one I've seen on Facebook?"

"She's OK for now." His body language spoke of indifference.

"You are what you were. There you were at thirteen surrounded by appalling people doing dreadful things to children. What values did you grow up with?"

Again, he shrugged his shoulders. "I use whatever situation I'm in to my own advantage. I was in my little bubble. Still am."

"But you know what happens to bubbles. Pop. They disappear. It's a wonder you haven't been to prison."

"I have. Two years. Fraud and money-laundering. I used that, too. Learned a lot. Learned how to use the prison system. Anyone who's been to prison learns how to be better at committing crimes. I used to drive the prison minibuses. Got out a lot. Went home. I had some dental work done and infection set in, didn't it, so I had to spend time at home convalescing. Cost me £10,000 that did and nothing was done to my teeth. Look me up. I hold the record for the most points on a driving licence and still driving."

"How do you manage that?"

"Appeals. Don't like driving now, though. If I get an idea, I lose concentration and forget what I'm doing.

"No one knows how I got to be what I am now. If I hadn't been to Crookham, I can't imagine it'd be the same. Nothing can hurt me. I'm in my bubble."

Gideon was a man of few words. He said what needed to be said and then stopped. He used "didn't it?" and "wasn't it?" between many brief sentences as though what he was saying was self-evident, even though he realised that he was describing unusual events in a life removed from most people's idea of reality. Maybe this gave his revelations sufficient normality for him. There was little eye contact. He did not reflect or elaborate; there were no pauses for thought; there was no self-doubt. His eyes shifted, taking in the totality of wherever he was, as if constantly looking for danger.

He tapped his phone.

"They're outside."

Gideon had nothing to hide now. There he was thirty years on. Cars, houses, travel, money, women, they were all around him and more or less unimportant. He was a wealthy man. "When I get it, I'm not interested. It's just the getting that I'm interested in." He had seen it all from as far back as he could remember, how people used people, and he had taken it on board. In his late forties, he had it all and had nothing. I admired his candour. He was right. Nothing could touch him. Nothing had changed. That's how he had managed to survive Crookham. He had paid a price. He was without a moral compass. It was not something he missed. He had no use for it. He, too, was a victim of Crookham Court School. "You can use my real name when you write about me. I don't mind. Nothing and no one can hurt me." He was absolutely right. The human being inside me, however, has kept his name withheld.

Now, in retrospect, it seems so obvious, children being cultivated. The warning signs were practically flashing, but at that time, no one made the connection. How could we have been so blind then when now it would be the first thought? We had no idea of the powerful drive behind sexual abuse, how the perpetrator's entire life is directed to this single end. It is an obsession; an addiction. Maybe it could all have ended that summer's day in 1983 when Gideon had a momentary tipping point and could have told me everything. Maybe not. Another six years were to pass, during which terrible crimes were committed before I finally realised the depravity of Crookham Court School. And it was a child's voice that revealed it.

TEN

Tipping points

In my experience, there comes a moment in the life of an abused child at which the guilt and shame become too much to bear alone. For Peter in 1989, this was the moment when he realised that his brother had been sexually abused and he wrote to Childline to get something done. The exposé on Esther Rantzen's *That's Life!* was the highest-profile televised institutionalised child abuse scandal in Britain. It was to see the law on how child victims are treated in court changed. It led to the Children Act being changed as it passed through Parliament. It alerted the public to a crime that few had thought about before. And it started a chain of events that just went on and on.

By 1988 my disillusionment with the school was such that I taught just a few lessons a week and assumed no one had any interest in this disgrace to the teaching profession. I came in just to see if there was anything I could learn to finish it off. I had no allies among the staff. I felt I was the only one who saw it as pernicious. The previous year, the school had hired a young undergraduate from Eton as a gap-year assistant. Freddie Browne (not his real name) was suspicious of one of the teachers, his close relationship with several boys and, he told me, some literature he carried in his briefcase. Freddie was not one to let niceties of morality stand in the way of his finding the truth. He was invited back a year after leaving the school to see a play directed by the very teacher about whom he harboured suspicions. While the play was being performed and its director was otherwise occupied, he entered his room and managed to pick open one of the twin locks of the briefcase just enough to slide his hand through the narrow opening and extract a brown envelope. He phoned me in a state of agitation. I collected him from the school and drove him to my home.

In my office, we peeled the bulky envelope open and spilled the contents onto a table. It was a collection of written material, handwritten and typed, drawings and photographs. The writings were in the first person and about how to punish, humiliate, and torture adolescent boys. The drawings were of these humiliations being put into practice. The photographs were of naked young men. My hands shook as I put each page on the plate of my photocopier and fumbled for which button to press. I had never seen anything like this before. Freddie replaced the envelope and returned them whence they had come.

We knew we had stumbled on something of significance, but were at a loss to know what to do with it. None of the boys in the photographs was at the school; no names of boys at the school were mentioned in the handwritten pieces. What we had read and the drawings we had seen were the product of a man's imagination. They were twisted and disgusting, describing cruelty and degradation, but they were, so far as we could tell, fiction. Should we be the thought police? Could the man be punished for having perverted ideas in his head? We had no evidence that any of what was described was being practised. There was also the question of how the documents had been obtained. The copied papers in my possession were the result of a theft.

I could take them to the man who was the headmaster at the time. I would have to tell him how they were obtained and I had the feeling that he would take the view that they were simply the outpourings of an over-inventive imagination. When the school closed that was exactly how he reacted when he saw the writings. The headmaster himself was not averse to beating the boys and arranged sessions of physical humiliation in front of the entire school as a way of maintaining order.

"The material" as it later became known was clearly of significance. Both of us knew that Crookham Court was unstable and that there would be a conclusion of some sort, but had no idea what form the denouement would take. In the meantime, we would wait and see.

ELEVEN

That's Life!

The wait was not a long one. In early 1989, a parent who was in the police force withdrew his son, made a complaint to the local police and Cadman was arrested. Police officers interviewed a number of boys inside the school. Nothing relating to any sexual matters was disclosed to them. Cadman was kept in custody overnight and released without charge the following day. A number of parents demanded a meeting and this was duly held in March. Unsurprisingly, disquiet was expressed and Cadman was given a number of demands. It was like the Chequers meeting twelve years before. The first of the demands was that Cadman's flat should be out-of-bounds to all boys at all times. Cadman flatly rejected that. There was no way forward. The meeting was over. Cadman continued.

It was a few weeks later that Peter contacted ChildLine and Esther asked one of the senior producers on *That's Life!* to investigate. Richard Woolfe knew that the reason the police investigations had revealed nothing was that the interviews with the boys had taken place inside the school. He spoke to staff at the school, discovered the names of those thought to be at risk and, with the permission of the parents, a number of children were taken to a place of safety and given the chance to talk there. Several did.

Esther visited with Richard and Hereward Harrison. She had chosen her day carefully knowing that Cadman would never permit her on the premises. The headmaster, Michael Gold, had told her that Cadman had to go to court in Reading to get an injunction against him and would be away for several hours. They arrived on a beautiful spring morning. "Deus ex Mercedes," I thought. The boys had been assembled in the main hall downstairs. Shafts of sunshine picked up flecks of dust, illuminating every corner. Esther wore a white jacket and a yellow patterned skirt. Everything was light and fresh; the familiar fixtures highlighted with a sudden clarity. For just a few hours Cadman had gone and with him the incubus of gloom.

"None of them met my eyes," Esther said years later. "They all knew."

(Meeting at Crookham Court School, May 1989): The audience fell silent. "Imagine you are in a meadow, a lovely green meadow." The boys imagined. "And then you step into the biggest, the smelliest cowpat you've ever seen." There were stifled giggles. "And you are so smelly and so 'orrible that you think you'll never be clean and everyone will see how dirty you are. But then you take a long hot bath and there you are. Clean. You can get rid of it. You really can. It's not you that smells. It's the cowpat. You can get rid of that horrible thing." The metaphor was not lost on any of them. Esther handed out some ChildLine leaflets and stickers and the boys scampered away like puppies.

"They went up to Cadman's flat," she said. "And plastered it with ChildLine stickers."

Of all the characters in this drama, Cadman was the one person Esther never did meet. By the time he returned to see the boys' handiwork, she had gone. For me, post-Cadman Crookham Court had been always winter and never Christmas. Now it felt as if spring really was arriving.

"We needed five disclosures," Esther told me later. "Five and then we could go ahead, but I spoke to John Birt first." John Birt was to become director-general of the BBC. "We were making very serious allegations and didn't want to be accused of 'trial by television'."

On three successive Sundays in June 1989, *That's Life!* broadcast the Crookham Court story to the nation and declared that Cadman was an abuser.

The teacher who was the author of the documents and had become the headmaster's right-hand man offered his services to the TV researchers. It was at this point that I gave "the material" simultaneously to the TV team and the police.

The documents had come from the briefcase of Alex Standish—a young teacher in his mid-twenties. He dressed formally with a jacket and tie or in his army uniform. He was in charge of the army cadet force group at the school. He was round-faced and spoke in a clipped accent. He hinted that he had an interesting past connected with a Russian ancestry. His self-importance was risible. He took it on himself to help run the school and allied himself with the headmaster of the day. He often had a small group of boys in his flat.

Esther's colleagues were far more experienced than me in the ways of abusers. They started investigating several other teachers in addition to Cadman and the author of the documents was one of those who came under the spotlight. We looked at which of the boys were his favourites and one name stood out. He appeared to be a chosen one and I was asked to interview him. My contact with Jacob Steele (not his real name) continued after the trial and the conviction of Cadman and two other teachers.

Jacob looked as if he would attract the attentions of a paedophile. He was good-looking and had a sporty physique. He also showed no sign of ever having been sexually abused. The more I came to know him, the more open he became and I had no reason to suspect that he was being other than honest with me. He had been in the master's room frequently, had smoked, had drunk alcohol and had been kissed on the forehead, he told me. He had been in the army cadet force at the school and had on one occasion had his trousers and pants removed and his genitalia had been shaved. The master had asked to see what had been done and Jacob had stood in front of him naked from the waist down. He had no self-consciousness and, at the time, thought it a reasonable request. When he had been naughty, he also thought it reasonable that the teacher had asked him to strip naked from the waist down and be caned.

On another occasion in the cadets, he had again been stripped, his penis covered with lipstick and sucked by an officer in charge. Word was, it had been arranged and paid for by a teacher.

Jacob was a boy whose relationship with his own father was so distant as to be non-existent and he saw the paternal affection he lacked in the kindness of this teacher. He appreciated the attention, enjoyed the holidays he had taken with him and affirmed that, although the man had seen him dress and undress, he had never been touched.

It was clear to me that this handsome young man had been the object of the teacher's affection, yet had never been touched by him; he may have been the subject of the writings and drawings, but had never been humiliated.

In 1991, Jacob volunteered to write a letter to the Department for Education and to give a statement to the police about his experiences. He affirmed that he gave the statement of his own free will.

The teacher went to teach elsewhere when Crookham Court School closed. That someone with such predilections and authorial interests was probably unsuited to teaching children was clear enough, but no crime had been committed and none of us was able to do anything.

From the single copy of "the material" I had made, I made two more copies. I gave one to Richard Woolfe and one to the local police. I made no other copies. The *That's Life!* copy remained with Richard Woolfe. A year later, I was incredulous to find that "the material" had come into the possession of Mirror Group Newspapers. They published an article on the front page of the *Sunday Mirror* in 1990 denouncing Standish as a sex pervert and criticising Esther for not telling the school he went to about him. There was, of course, nothing to tell and, as for his being a sex pervert, that was more than we knew. Both sued the publishers and both won their cases. Esther was awarded a quarter of a million pounds and the teacher one penny. Esther's award was reduced on appeal and was eaten up by costs. She donated £25,000 to ChildLine. The teacher may have considered his penny a victory of sorts. I never have discovered if or how he received the coin.

"It was an awful experience," Esther told me. "And all such a waste. I told the editor that we were investigating a possible paedophile ring and that this would be jeopardised if they went ahead with the story."

Almost a quarter of a century was to pass before I knew exactly how I had been misled and just how this paedophile had operated. Paedophiles are very clever people and this one was no exception. Nothing was what it had seemed to be. One of the pages I had copied was headed "Training Andrew". It was a clue all of us had missed.

Throughout this time another man who had been a boy at Crookham Court School from 1987 to 1989 was keeping a secret that was slowly tearing him to pieces. It had already cost him his first wife and child. He could see that he would lose his second family unless he spoke out.

"It was the nightmares I couldn't stand," he was to tell me. "I kept hearing his voice telling me, 'You'll never forget that your first time was with me,' and he was right. I never have forgotten. I can't get that voice out of my head."

His tipping point came in the early hours of 16 December 2009. I turned on my computer to start my morning's work.

A small and, at that time, unfamiliar, icon winked at me to show me that I had received a Facebook message. I clicked it.

> Not sure if you can remember me but I was at Crookham from 86–89 and I was in your english class for a lot of the time apart from when you used to throw me out for un rully behaviour.
>
> Well first of all I would like to appoligide for that and maybe after reading the rest of this letter you will understand why.
>
> When I caame to crokkham I was a happy go lucky child who had learning problems ie dyslexia.
>
> I was doing fine till one day alex standish become my tutor. From then on my life went down hill.
>
> For me Crookham has never ended I live with the nightmares everyday and night because of what that so called teacher did to me.
>
> The papers were right about him. You should have more recognision for what you did but her got the glory, well in my eyes he is a predertor just like cadman and the rest of those scum.
>
> You might be wondering why I am writing to you telling you this after all these years, well its quite simple … I know I can trust you and maybe just maybe you might know someone on the police force that delt with Crookham.
>
> I am still scared of standish cause in my eyes he is still a very powerful man and has very powerful friends. I have asked people I know in the services about one of his old jobs which was editor of janes inteligence weekly and you dont get that job unless you have been with one of the services. If you look at his entry on wikI he has had some very powerful jobs and I am scared that if I go to the police he will use those resourses against me.

I want to go to the police but I am scared for my wife and kids will be draggged into this.

Please help as I dont know what else to do.

I am sorry for dropping this on you but I feel like I have no one else to turrn to that will understand what happened back then.

I replied instantly:

"Please call me on 01X or 07X and please know that I am going to be with you all the way. (I'm at the theatre with my sons this morning from 09.30 to 12.00). You have no reason to feel guilty."

When we spoke, I said: "You must do two things. One—tell your family, and two—tell the police. If you like, I'll come and see you."

In fact, he had already disclosed to the police, but he said that, yes, he would like me to come and see him. He was true to his word and on 2 January 2010, I drove to Brighton. He told me he would meet me in his road as, although his wife knew that I was coming, he didn't want her involved. It became clear from his several calls to her on his mobile that she had got herself to the stage of suspecting that any man from Crookham Court might wish to do her husband some harm.

He was the "Andrew" of "the material". Andy Hudson—his real name, used at his request—was dressed for business in a white shirt, dark suit, and tie. He carried a briefcase and several loose files. He climbed into the passenger seat. We shook hands formally. I would have recognised him in the street—the small cheeky face, still boyish, bright eyes, and teeth that needed specialist care. The skin around the eyes was creased and spoke of stress and late nights.

(Conversation, 2 January 2010): "Look, Andy, this meeting is likely to end up in court, so the line I'm going to take with you is how you're coping with all this. You'll tell me what happened—and you can be as frank as you like. I'll let you talk and I won't say anything, except about the effect it's having on you now. I absolutely can't put words into your mouth so, although every fibre of my being wants to put an arm around you and tell you that what you went through was awful, dreadful, and any other adjective you can think of and that no one should have to undergo such pain, I can't and won't. You understand? OK. Is there a country house restaurant or somewhere we can go?"

Andy was not a frequenter of such places, so we ended up in a car park with the brilliant winter sunshine streaming in through the glass roof of my car.

"We might even get approached by the police," he said. "This is where the gays hang out."

He told me his story factually, clinically, and precisely. He remembered every detail, every intimate action and how his body responded. I wanted to cry for his pain, for the loss of his innocence, for the intrusion that went to the very core of his being.

I had to be correct and distant. I listened and did not respond. Standish had been his tutor and, as such, was responsible for the administration of his pocket money. Andy collected it weekly from Standish. At some point, Standish told him he was unable to administer it himself and that he should go to another teacher, Dr. Printer, who, unlike him, had a car and could collect money from the bank easily. Andy went to Printer for his money and saw that sometimes no amount was written down. He took increasingly large amounts without any objection being made and soon knew that he had exceeded his allowance. He spent the money on cigarettes. After some time, Standish had approached him and told him he had checked his account and that he owed hundreds of pounds over and above his allowance. Should Standish get the money from Andy's father? Andy had panicked and knew his father would be furious at the overspend and know what it had been squandered on. He feared his father's anger. Standish invited him to spend some time thinking of possible alternative solutions and that Andy should speak to him again. Andy came up with nothing. A few days later, Standish suggested some harsh physical exercises in his room so that the pain would be a punishment. Andy readily agreed and presented himself in PE kit for the exercises. Standish told him that the amount owed was decreasing each time. He also told him he would be exercising until he was an old man unless he, Andy, thought of a way to pay the debt off more quickly.

"He said I could pay off my debts more quickly if I did the exercises naked, so I undressed. I did the star jumps he told me to do and everything was flopping around—penis, balls, everything. He was looking and I could tell he liked it."

He paused. There he was. Fourteen. A child naked and vulnerable in front of a teacher. A teacher who had responsibility for his welfare and had the trust of his parents.

"I used to have to do my prep at a desk outside his room. I'd sit there in my PE kit and he'd call me into his room. After a while, I'd just strip naked before he told me. Every time, I'd have everything out. One night, I came with an injury to the top of my leg. Standish saw it and made me sit on his lap. He gently stroked my leg and his fingers moved up to my groin and then gently onto my penis."

He looked down. I wanted to interject and tell him not to be ashamed, that it wasn't his fault, it was his body, his physiological response to what was happening, but he had to get it out in his way. His facial expression tensed. There we sat, in my car overlooking the sea on that bright January morning, and this shy young man was about to tell me the thing that had preyed on his mind for more than two decades.

"I was quite undeveloped. I didn't have pubic hair or anything like that. When he touched my penis, it became hard. He seemed pleased and said, 'We can't waste that.' He masturbated me and something happened to my body. It was like an orgasm. Nothing came out. I was too young. It was a dry orgasm."

Andy finished telling me his story in that Brighton car park. Later he wrote down what happened after his dry orgasm (email, 1 May 2012):

> A few days later Standish called me up to his room but this time he just told me to drop my trousers and bend over the chair. I assumed the position and waited. WHACK—the first blow stung like nothing before and I was soon crying. I turned around to see a clothes or hair brush in his hand. He hit me again, this time harder still and I couldn't contain the yelp of pain. He told me to shut up. He hit me a few times more and told me to get out. I ran to my dorm but as I opened the door I could hear other people in there, so I ran down the back stairs and out of the back door and towards the swimming pool. I sat on the stairs and cried and cried. I was in pain and I didn't know what I had done to deserve that beating.
>
> The next day I saw Standish and he treated me like any other pupil at the school as if nothing had happened. Later that day he told me I could start doing my homework in my dorm a few nights a week if I was good and my work came up to standard. I worked really hard those few days as I was desperate to knuckle down and try and pass my exams.
>
> About a week or so later, Standish told me to report to his room after prep. I was relaxed as I knocked on his door as I had been working hard and I hadn't got into trouble. I sat down and he told me I could smoke if I wanted to. He then told me I had paid off most of the money now and I only had to do a few PT sessions and it was all paid back. I felt a huge wave or relief wash over me.
>
> We talked that night about a few different things, but never once did he mention the beatings or anything

else. It was as if nothing had happened. At that point, he started to tell me about what had happened to him before he was a teacher at Crookham. He told me he had been on holiday with a friend to Finland and had crossed over the border into the Soviet Union by mistake whilst out skiing. They had been caught and treated like spies and were handed over to the KGB and tortured by them for a few weeks until they were expelled from the country. He said that it had left him mentally scarred and with mental health problems. He told me about some of the torture he endured and I felt so sorry for him that night. I stopped hating him, or so I thought.

A few nights later, he called me back into his room and this time I knew I was in trouble as I had been kicked out of chemistry for trying to mix a few chemicals up to see what would happen.

I was right. He was furious with me. He told me to bend over the chair and he whacked me with the hair brush again. I got 6 whacks that night and every one of them stung like mad and I cried and cried. Afterwards he told me sit on his lap. He gave a cuddle and said he didn't want to hurt me but I had to learn right from wrong. He gave me a tissue to dry my eyes and blow my nose. He then started to touch me again. Again I just froze and closed my eyes and wished it over so I could leave. Soon it was over and I was out of there. I just thought it was my fault and I tried the next day to be good. I even tried to say sorry to the chemistry teacher but I think by then she had given up on me and told me from now on I was to sit at the back and do lines.

I gave up learning. What the hell was the point, I thought? Even when I tried it got me nowhere. I hated the place and soon the anger was back and soon I was always in trouble for being a little shit.

Later that term Standish called me up to his room and as soon as I walked in I just pulled down my trousers and leant over the chair. I knew at this point I didn't come into this room unless I was in trouble. He walked towards me. I just closed my eyes and tried to think of anything but what was just about to happen to me.

I felt his hand on the lower part of my back … oh shit I thought … he is going to actually cane me and is going to hold me down. I closed my eyes tightly. All of a sudden I felt this immense pain in my bum and I pulled away and I looked down and saw a hair brush in his hand. He just smiled at me and said, "Oh well, you aren't ready for that then. Get dressed and get out."

I pulled up my pants and trousers as quickly as I could and ran out of that room. My bum stung and I winced with the pain. I ran to the nearest toilet, locked the door and pulled down my trousers and pants and grabbed some toilet roll and wiped my bum. Blood. I started crying. What was happening to me? I sat on that toilet until I stopped bleeding, but I pushed some paper between my bum cheeks that night as I went to sleep just in case. That night I just lay there crying and wishing I could go back home.

That morning I got up so quick and ran to the toilets wincing with pain once more. Went into a cubicle and checked the toilet roll I had put there the night before. My bum had bled a bit during the night. I sat down and tried to go to the toilet and found it was too painful. I flushed the chain and went for a wash, walking a bit funny as it hurt so much to walk.

As I went for breakfast I knew I wasn't going to be able to sit down properly and panicked … oh my god if I can't sit down then what am I going to do at class time … I knew I had to sit down and get on with it. I was right as

I sat down with my breakfast it hurt so much I wanted to cry but I knew I couldn't.

That day was a blur of pain and going to the toilet to check there was no more bleeding. It took a few days for the pain to stop and the whole time I couldn't go to the toilet as it hurt too much.

TWELVE

The Standish trial

We next met at the Crown Court in Reading which opened on 6 February 2012.

Judge Stephen John's instructions to the jury were crisp: use the judgment you use in your everyday lives. In this case there isn't a question that it might have been done by someone else. It is a question of whether this party is telling the truth, or the other party is telling the truth. You have to assess which one you believe.

The prosecution's case reduced the subtleties to facts and the emotions to zero. Andrew Hudson was a boy at Crookham Court School from 1986 until 1989. During this time, he had Alex Standish as his tutor and later his guardian. Mr. Standish isolated Andrew Hudson from his friends. He groomed him, created a scenario in which he had a hold over him, led him through levels of manipulation to a point at which he had him under his control and repeated abuse took place. He isolated him by making him do his prep at a desk placed outside his bed-sitting room away from every other boy. He then told him that he owed the school a large sum of pocket money. He threatened to tell his father. When Andy responded that he did not want his father to know as he would be angry with him, Mr. Standish invited Andy to think of ways in which this money could be paid back. In the absence of any workable ideas, Mr. Standish suggested physical exercises. These took place during the prep period when he was taken from the desk outside his room. As this desk was isolated, no one noticed his absence. He was rewarded with beer and cigarettes. These were later accompanied by cuddles. The exercises carried on, but still the debt was not being repaid in full. How helpful of Mr. Standish to suggest to the boy that he might pay it off more quickly, simply by taking off his clothes. How exciting Mr. Standish found it to see the boy's genitalia move and how he loved being in control of his naked body. One day, he saw an injury on his leg. He invited Andy to sit with him on his chair so he could stroke it and move his hands upwards to his penis and he found he could make it grow. Masturbation, orgasm, then some sadism—beating—and the insertion of an object, a hairbrush into Andy's anus.

The defence's case was that it did not happen; that it could not have happened. There was no desk outside the room. Hudson did his prep with other boys under the control of a prefect who would have noticed his absence. At the time in question, a school production of the musical *Oliver* was being performed in the area outside the bedsit, so prep could not have taken place there. So convinced was the defence that it could not have happened that counsel wondered how the judge could possibly direct the jury and invited him to finish the proceedings, an offer the judge declined.

The prosecution paraded witnesses who were boys at the time. They told not of the evil of Standish, but of his wonderfulness. "Without him, I wouldn't be where I am today." The defence brought forward other boys, now middle-aged men, who echoed these themes, who all remembered the production of *Oliver* that happened during prep and were certain that there was no desk up there on the minstrel's gallery outside the bedsit, and who testified to the marvel of the man, Standish. Yes, he could be familiar with them, but he was their friend.

Then it was Andy's turn. He was heard from behind a screen. He put the unthinkable, the unbearable into words. He had been isolated from the other boys, taken into Standish's study, made to strip naked and be humiliated with physical exercises on many occasions, regularly masturbated to orgasm, beaten, and raped with a hairbrush. When the defence put it to him that it was an invention that could not have happened, he was resolute and repeated himself, cracking just once when the defence counsel insisted that nothing had happened—"Were you there?" he spat. And the money that was owed, this huge sum, £250, £300. There was no proof. The pocket money records that had survived from the time showed a small overspend. The record on such and such a day showed this small amount taken, on another day, this amount, and so on and on. The defence went through these detailed records, emphasising Standish's punctilious attention to detail. "I'll take your word for it," was the reply on each occasion as the defence reiterated dates and amounts from the record. "I'll take your word for it." "Don't take learned counsel's word for it, Mr. Hudson. This is your opportunity to respond," the judge interjected. But here was not a thirty-eight-year-old man facing the demolition of his veracity. A fourteen-year-old boy awed by immutable authority was replying. Andy Hudson was back in his schooldays. Of course he believed what the imposing figure in wig and robe was telling him. He was the master of the situation, all the facts at his disposal. Andy had simply to acquiesce as he had all those years ago. The facts were as fictitious now as they had been then. The money had not existed. The debt was a pretext for control.

The trial revealed how, all those years ago, I had been interviewing the wrong boy. Jacob was the boy Standish wanted to have, but dared not. Instead he had Andy and how he hated him for not being Jacob.

"Andy," I said to him in one of his darker moments, "in your case, it's like finding out how a magician creates an illusion.

You need to know how you were tricked. In understanding it, you will be able to forgive yourself."

I sent the transcript to another boy who told me he had been propositioned by Standish. "Maybe the revelation of how he inveigled his way into people's lives will help you see that there is less to him than meets the eye."

Alex Standish came across as a confident figure in the Reading courtroom. He wore a blue suit and appeared slimmer than he had been. His pomposity had not changed one jot. He assured the jury that all this talk of beer and cigarettes was nonsense. He could stand neither. He only ever drank wine. So assured was he that he preceded one of his answers to prosecuting counsel with the words, "The problem you have, Mr. Branston, is ..." Quite what problem prosecuting counsel had we were not to find out. Judge John suggested that the defendant would not help himself by talking to learned counsel in this way. Standish's problem was (1) that he was full of himself and (2) that his defence was being meticulously unpicked detail by detail by a brilliant and forensic mind. It was during questioning, for example, that it came out that Standish had written a book about Crookham Court School. He titled it *Suffer Little Children*. Standish seemed rather proud of being a writer. As it was unpublished, the manuscript was taken by the police and the prosecution read it overnight. "May I refer you to page 74, Mr. Standish?" prosecuting counsel asked. He read, "Mr. Cadman took me to The Falmouth Arms. As usual we arrived late and he just had enough time to order two pints." "Lemonade, Mr. Standish? It may well be that you preferred fine wine, but you'd drink beer when you had to."

Gareth Branston's closing speech (reproduced with his permission and with only the boys' names changed) is a succinct account of one paedophile's modus operandi and is an education in how easily it can happen:

What did Alex Standish offer at Crookham Court in the late 1980s? He offered kindness. He offered a place to go. He offered a spare key for his tutor group; a place perhaps to smoke according to Andrew Hudson … certainly to drink alcohol. The defendant admits as much in his interview. Alex Standish offered a place to read; a place to escape with a teacher who was perhaps younger than many of those at Crookham Court; a place to read books and to borrow books; some you might think quite scandalous.

There were trips to the National Liberal Club with the teacher. Money spent on them, on fine dinners. He was kind. He was nice. He instinctively knew what his group liked and he would spend time with them. There was more of course. We know from what Jacob Steele had to say in 1990/91 that there were foot massages, shoulder and neck massages, play fights, kisses on the forehead, hugs and little shows of affection that made things comfortable for his boys.

Of course, this is not to say that Alex Standish indecently assaulted all of the boys in his charge. Far from it; I do not say that for a moment. He was not Dr. William Printer. He was not Philip Cadman. What we need to remember perhaps is that Mr. Standish was still fairly young at this time. He was twenty-three, twenty-four, or twenty-five. He was still nine or ten years older than the boys that we are concerned with, but still relatively young. There is nothing to suggest that he had acted on his sexual interest in young boys before. In fact, it is perhaps safe to say that he would not have been as well practised as those older teachers who had been about much longer.

Perhaps Alex Standish was not quite so brave. He was not someone who had been getting away with it for some time at Crookham Court. It is quite clear that others had been getting away with it for quite some time without anyone—Alex Standish included—blowing the whistle. He was not someone perhaps who felt as confident in those kinds of actions. This was his first job in such an environment surrounded by boys after university. He was a man admittedly confused in his own sexuality. This was almost certainly, the Crown would say, his first venture into this kind of activity and it would inevitably start slowly. But we do know, of course, that he had a sexual interest in some in his care. He admits as much in his interview. A direct question into whether he was sexually attracted to boys at the time and a response in the affirmative. There was an explanation, a qualification to that answer a little later, but a positive admission nonetheless. What is more, he goes on.

Jacob Steele: perhaps he is the one. Classically attractive, as he puts it. Jacob Steele: the object of his interest. Perhaps Jacob Steele was his first object of lust. Jacob Steele received foot massages. Jacob Steele received a shoulder massage. Jacob Steele was hugged. He was kissed on the forehead. He was punished too: caning, three times, the third time with his pants and his trousers down. We know that later, from what Jacob Steele had to say nearer the time, that Alex Standish had an interest in seeing his genitalia when they had been shaved in that Territorial Army initiation rite.

There is talk also, of course, with Jacob Steele of masturbation; talk of shaving other young people and that kind of thing and paying for others to be shaved. All those things that Jacob Steele talks about in the letter, parts of which I read out to him. There are all those things in his statement from 1991; the things he claims now did not happen or some of the things he claims did not happen. He claims now that somehow, somewhere, they were made up and that he signed a statement or wrote a letter but they must have been made up. Whose imagination did those activities come from? We have no idea.

What I would suggest is that they don't just come out of nowhere. They were not just figments of the imagination. When he protested very strongly on the screen, as you saw, he sounded perhaps just a little bit like a child again; a child who knows he has said a bit too much and wants to put it all back in the bottle. Oh yes, there was a sexual interest from Alex Standish the teacher at the time towards young Jacob Steele.

Jacob Steele would have been nine years younger than Alex Standish. Alex Standish started at the school when he was twenty-three and finished when he was twenty-five. Did Alex Standish act upon that interest? Was he brave enough to take his first steps in that direction? Well, maybe not. Perhaps Jacob Steele was too strong a character for that, too immune from Mr. Standish's gentle and inquisitive forays. Perhaps Jacob Steele was too much of a risk. He was a classically attractive boy; one of the beautiful people perhaps, one of the popular crowd at school perhaps; a presence at the school; well liked with lots of friends. Not Jacob Steele, Mr. Standish thinks. Look at Jacob Steele; admire Jacob Steele; remain close to him; but touching would be unlikely to be tolerated and might indeed be disastrous. Alex Standish was not ready for that yet.

So who does this teacher turn to? Well, he does what every paedophile does. He looks for the vulnerable. He looks for the isolated and the one least likely to have friends to tell; the one least likely to be able to object and to challenge him. He looks at Andrew Hudson, a boy who struggles academically at school, a boy who is bullied and a boy who does not have many friends and who is already isolated to an extent. How does he proceed, Mr. Standish?

Well, he isolates him further. How can he do this? Because he is a man in authority. He is looking for the vulnerable from a position of power or authority over this lad.

First, he is a teacher. Secondly, and more than that, he is Andrew's tutor. Thirdly, he is master of boarding. Fourthly, he is deputy head. Fifthly, he is head of the Army Cadets. Finally, he is his guardian. I wonder, have we dispensed with all the silliness now about whether this defendant was the legal guardian to Andrew or not? It seems to have taken up a lot of time. There were a number of questions and matters of dispute put to Andrew on behalf of Mr. Standish. Maybe no documents were signed; maybe there is no power of attorney. It is quite clear, is it not, that Andrew was told that Alex Standish was his guardian? It is quite clear that he was told that by his parents. It is quite clear that Keith Hudson believed that to be so; that the guardianship was done on a handshake. Of course, it is quite clear that Alex Standish asserted that and acted in that position. He signs police statements as guardian, agreeing with the police that he was the guardian. He described Andrew Hudson as one of his three wards in that letter of 3rd February 1989 which we talked about towards the end of yesterday.

Alex Standish was in a position of great authority over Andrew Hudson. More than that though, it was not just his position. You have seen the type of person that Alex Standish is. Is he shy, retiring, timid, nervous, and the sort that people in class could easily get away with murder around? Or is he absolutely confident, sure of himself, and in control of the situation, ready to point out to the poor barrister who has to ask him questions that "The problem you've got, Mr. Branston, is this"? Did we get a flavour of Alex Standish the teacher yesterday: the power and the authority that he is used to exerting upon others? If that is so in the Crown Court when he is being tried for serious offences, how much more of that was there in him when he was in command of young, impressionable boys who were in his care?

So this is a man with a huge amount of authority and influence. What has he done with Andrew Hudson? Well, he has shown him kindness. There was a willingness to allow him some slack. But when he makes demands of course, the master of boarding is going to be obeyed.

But it is not enough, of course, to have Andrew Hudson doing his homework outside of your study. That does not achieve what you want to achieve. Just being poor in work is probably not going to let Mr. Standish act upon his impulses and so there needs to be something more. There needs to be a situation devised. The other boys might not be so gullible. They might not believe what you say. But Andrew, the vulnerable boy, would.

So we have the device of the pocket money situation constructed. I don't know how much planning went into that at all. We really cannot tell because we only have the records that Mr. Standish has chosen to provide us with and the explanation that he gives for them may have to be taken with a rather large pinch of salt. But we do know from Andrew that he was told that he owed a great deal of money.

Do you remember when Andrew was being cross-examined by Mr. Barlow? He used a phrase several times. He said to Mr. Barlow, "I'll take your word for it. I'll take your word for it. I'll take your word for it." I think His Honour had to interject and make clear that he should not just take Mr. Barlow's word for it; he should consider it, think about it, and see whether he knows the answer. Wasn't that rather indicative? That was a thirty-eight-year-old man, faced with someone apparently with knowledge about his life, perhaps even someone he regarded as being in authority, putting things to him about dates and places and events and the like. "I'll take your word for it," he said. He was not challenging it. He was taking Mr. Barlow's word for it.

Let us rewind quickly twenty-four years to a boy of fourteen faced with his tutor/teacher telling him he owed £250 or £300. He does not challenge Mr. Barlow who is there to cross-examine him, and he knows he is there to cross-examine him. Is he really going to challenge Alex Standish, when he knew in fact, of course, that he had been taking advantage of the system? They had discovered what seemed to be a loophole that nobody was really keeping tabs, so that when he went to Dr. Printer (because Mr. Standish was away) nobody really seemed to be noting anything down. He knows he has probably taken more than he should and now he's been caught and he's in the spotlight—that teacher's glare.

I imagine we have all had that as children at school. Even when we have not done something wrong but there is a teacher there looking for someone who has done something wrong—perhaps accusing—there is the fear, the feeling that "Maybe I did do something wrong; I didn't think I did something wrong but maybe I did, I don't know." The teacher's glare is all-powerful when you are quite young, and doubly so you might think in someone who was particularly vulnerable, isolated, and bullied.

Andrew Hudson was most probably overdrawn and Mr. Standish would only know how much if he had proper records. But of course finding that exact figure does not matter. What does matter is what Andrew Hudson had to say. He was told that he had taken the money, and a lot of it. That was something that frightened Andrew Hudson. He was worried about his parents finding out and wanted to get it paid off as soon as possible. There was none of this rubbish about, "I'll get £30 or £40 off my parents by the end of the term." That is so inconsistent with what you heard from Keith Hudson and what you would understand the situation to be. Andrew Hudson was fearful of his parents finding out.

Basically he is in Alex Standish's study now and he is being accused in his eyes of theft. It is obvious what is coming next to Andrew Hudson, of course. He is a boy who is regularly in detention. His grades are low. He is punished. He will need to be disciplined. Is he? Well, no, not officially. According to the interview of Mr. Standish, not disciplined at all.

This is an environment where a strict beasting is the least that Andrew Hudson could expect. What happens next? Well, Alex Standish has the boy in his grasp at this point, doesn't he? What does he do? What does Mr. Standish do? As I say, he is not experienced like in this type of thing. He can't just grab the boy and fondle him. That really is not likely to work. It is certainly, you may think, moving a little too quickly. He cannot be sure how Andrew Hudson would react if he did that.

So what does Alex Standish do? Well, he pauses for thought. He lets Andrew think for a bit. "What are we going to do about this money that has gone? What are we going to do, you having taken all that money? How are you going to pay it back?" Perhaps the defendant was hoping that Andrew would come up with something sexual himself. Of course, it would not take him very long to realise that that was highly unlikely. So it is necessary for the defendant to take some action himself and come up with a punishment. That is what is expected. Again, part of being nice to Andrew and part of being something different from the environment outside—it is not quite the public beasting that Andrew expects. These circuits will be in private, in the defendant's room. Nobody else watching.

We know of course, indeed, that Alex Standish was in charge of discipline in the boarding house in the absence of Michael Gold, so there is no real shock that he is taking control here. We know from his book that an investigation into punishments did occur in his study.

So Andrew Hudson's punishments begin. The circuits; the PT kit; the exercises; all in accordance with expectations but all a bit "cushty", as Andrew Hudson described it. The water is being tested by Alex Standish. Not enough yet, so he adds a twist. Andrew is going to learn what it is like to steal. There is a punishment designed to make him feel embarrassed—naked, and the defendant just watching him. After it stops there is the offer of a cigarette. One of X's cigarettes, I think was the observation by Andrew Hudson. A little detail there that you might think is significant. An odd little detail to add if it is not true.

There is the assurance by his tutor that more of the money has been paid off. And so it goes on with the naked exercises, no doubt satisfying to some extent Alex Standish's urges towards young boys in his charge. Then there is a continuation of Alex Standish being nice to this boy. One day he sees that Andrew is struggling with a knee injury that we know he has. He tells him to sit down and have a cigarette. He shows concern. He looks at Andrew's knee. He examines it and he pats his lap for Andrew to come and sit down. There is nothing greatly unusual about that, you might think. This is a teacher who hugs and kisses his boys. The defendant looks at Andrew's knee and examines it, and when he finished he says, "Stay there, that feels nice." Then he gives him a cuddle and he touches him. He tests the water some more.

The next time, of course, he is getting is bit more brave. He is brave enough to go a bit further. This time he tickles the boy's groin and the fourteen-year-old boy gets an erection. "Well, we can't let that go to waste," says Alex Standish. That is a very specific memory from Andrew Hudson of words spoken. Alex Standish masturbates him to a dry orgasm, the boy still too young to ejaculate.

Now, a word or two about that incident. The defendant says that all of this is made up and that none of it happened. You might want to think on a few things here. Let us just imagine for a moment that Andrew Hudson, a thirty-eight-year-old man, was intent on making up such things all these years after he was at school. Let us imagine he was sophisticated enough to create a story, to talk about a teacher sexually assaulting him. What is he going to include in that story? Is he going to include the fact that he was aroused? Is that man going to make such an admission which, on the face of it, might suggest that he got some kind of enjoyment and pleasure out of that touching? We of course know, and many of you will understand, that that would be a physiological response to the type of touching this defendant did. But is Andrew Hudson, in coming up with a story, going to make that up, or is he going to say, "Well, this man fondled my penis for a while; I certainly wasn't aroused; I certainly wasn't erect"?

Secondly, in this story that he is creating against Alex Standish is he going to say he had an orgasm? Is the man who is making all of this up really going to say, "Well, I was so aroused that I had an orgasm"? That very definitely might suggest, you might think at first blush, that he enjoyed it in some way. It is easy for you to say that, even though of course again it is a physiological reaction to what was taking place. The person making this up is going to think, are they not, "Isn't that going to say that I enjoyed this? I am not doing this to say I enjoyed it; I am doing this to get Mr. Standish into trouble."

Thirdly on this point, the dry orgasm. We all understand what he means by that and he explains what he means by that. It is the fact that he had not proceeded far enough through puberty at that stage to ejaculate. Isn't that simply way too sophisticated for someone telling lies about this to distinguish between an earlier incident between the two of them of masturbation and a later one by reference to the fact that he had developed later so that he did ejaculate, but he didn't earlier? Why make that up? Why make that distinction? Isn't that a really rather extraordinary distinction to make or a detail to add if it were not a genuine memory on the part of Andrew?

Perhaps just as telling about that incident is Andrew's recollection that the defendant "tutted", as if he was disappointed. That is a very, very, very small detail but really rather telling, I would suggest. The points I have made here very much relate to Count 1 on your indictment, but very much also relate to Count 2. Of course, we know from Andrew that the masturbation continues. It happens again, regularly as he recalls but not every night. Sometimes it was taken as rather a broad-brush approach to dispute with Andrew that he was there every single night. He never said that. He always accepted that he wasn't there every night, but it seemed very often to him that he seemed very often to feel lonely when he had to work outside at the desk. It seemed very often when he was in his tutor's room dealing with these circuits. No doubt it dominated his recollection of that period of his life.

You might recall, of course, when asked a specific question about one single incident of masturbation, his recollection was that it seemed to go on for eternity. He was a young boy. His concept of time this far down the line is likely to be tricky. It did not happen every night. It happened regularly and it continued when Andrew was fifteen. You have then Count 2 and his description of what happened in Count 2 and how it differs from Count 1.

You will remember, as I told you at the beginning of the case, these counts are chosen as three specific examples and Count 4 as representative of the fact that these occurred on more than one occasion. There is no suggestion it only happened four times. It happened much more regularly than that, but we try to choose representative examples.

Count 2 is a specific example of when he was fifteen and he had that weird sensation where Mr. Standish was doing this to him, feeling that he had to go to the toilet, the defendant laughing and his first ejaculation. His recollection this time was that the defendant did not "tut" as if disappointed. The defendant was excited, telling him that he would remember that for the rest of his life, which of course we know he has. The defendant saying he was proud to say that it was him who did it.

Let us think again about that for a moment. Let us imagine that we are creating this story out of nothing about Mr. Standish and we want to get him into trouble. Whatever kind of grudge we have that makes us want to allege that he sexually abused us when we were children, what do you think of? Do you think of the actions that took place? Do you think of the places where it happened? Do you think of the reasons why you were there? You might come up with some words that the adult said, but how sophisticated do you have to be in your story making to include your first ejaculation as one of the incidents and the defendant's response as being one of pride?

We know after that things developed. The water had been well and truly tested by then and he moved on to other things in the autumn term, Andrew believes. They were harsher things. There was the smacking with the shoe; the telling him that he was a naughty boy. Of course, the defendant knows that this boy now is well and truly in his control. If what has previously occurred has taken place, nobody has been told and he feels safe and more confident. He is definitely past the point where Andrew is going to tell, if he was ever going to tell. He has not.

So a little of the sadistic sexual interest that the defendant has comes through. Why he has this interest we don't know, but it is obvious that many people in the world are indeed turned on by elements of sadistic sexual activity. Of course the hair brush comes out. A shoe was being used to smack and tell this boy, who is being punished, that he is a naughty boy. Then the hair brush comes out and it is used to smack him. But more than that, of course, it is used to insert into the boy's anus.

We are really going to extraordinary lengths here, aren't we? We are coming up with our story to get Mr. Standish into trouble. We are accusing him of sexually touching us when we were young. Where on earth are we getting this element from? Who decides in their false allegation that a hair brush is going to feature at all? And not just feature but be the object of such obvious humiliation. Who makes that up?

By all means, if you are coming up with this false allegation of sexual abuse, for whatever reason, if you have decided that you have it in for this person and you are going to make all this up, of course you might want to make it as serious as possible for them. You might want to suggest that the defendant tried to put his penis inside you; that he tried to have sex in that way. Isn't that the obvious next step in this false story? But a hair brush?

Then the reaction that Andrew Hudson describes; the soreness and the bleeding. That is probably obvious if you are thinking about it and you have got that far. But there is the embarrassment. He spoke of the feeling that people were looking at him. That really is quite something, isn't it? You might think it is vivid. The boy felt the after-effects of having that object put inside his bottom. It reminded him of what had happened when he was walking round the school afterwards. It made him think that others would notice somehow and would see what had happened, so he would be embarrassed.

Of course, if this account is all false once we have got the hair brush why doesn't the hair brush feature again and again? If we have got to that stage, why doesn't it carry on? It only happens the once. "You are obviously not ready for that," was Andrew's recollection of what Mr. Standish had to tell him. That is the hair brush of course that Andrew Hudson does not identify. He is shown a hair brush by the police in a later interview. He recognises it as a brush similar to one of the brushes that Mr. Standish had, but he never makes any suggestion that that brush was used in any way upon him. Wouldn't it have been the easiest thing in the world, once he recognised that brush, to say, "Ah yes, that was one of the brushes. There were other brushes: the wooden clothes brush I have mentioned and the black hair brush with the handle I have mentioned but, yes, that brush too." It would have been the easiest thing in the world for him to do that, but he didn't. He said, "No, that brush wasn't the one."

We know Mr. Standish did not try the hair brush in his bottom again. Maybe Mr. Standish realised he had gone too far that time. Maybe he was concerned that the boy might tell someone now about something that was so extraordinary and so painful for him. Maybe it was a sign of Mr. Standish's lack of experience in that type of matter in abusing boys in his care. As we have said, unlike Mr. Cadman, it was his first time and he backs off. Maybe he was biding his time until later; we don't know. Maybe it is an example of him being gentle in order to get what he wants. We don't want to scare the boy off now, do we?

So the masturbation continues but the hair brush does not. The defendant, therefore, with Andrew Hudson has taken his first steps in acting upon his impulses towards schoolboys. He is, no doubt, being fortified in those actions by the sort of environment that he has been working in. He knows that there is inappropriate behaviour going on involving other teachers from the beginning of his time there; of incidents that have essentially been hushed up, you might think. Certainly the authorities were not notified. No doubt there were rumours going to the very top, to Mr. Cadman the principal, and that story that Alex Standish relates in his book about the boy not being there at bedtime in his dorm, Mr. Cadman being challenged about it and the boy turning up in bed shortly afterwards. If he is getting away with such acts in that school there should not be any difficulty in Mr. Standish delving just a little bit into that particularly murky world.

Of course, this cannot last forever. The kind of chaos, the horror, the lack of control, and the sordid activity cannot proceed forever. Parents do find out. Matrons do find out. Headmasters do find out. Eventually we know, of course, that BBC consumer programmes do find out. But before that, things are said and people do eventually make a fuss. The police are considered and eventually they become involved.

When a fuss begins to be made at the beginning of January 1989, it presents quite a dilemma for Alex Standish, of course. I do not suppose he wanted the police involved particularly. Who knows what Andrew might say if he is questioned. But if the police are eventually going to come into the school, it is best to be there and best to be in control of the situation and to monitor and see what is happening.

So he takes the decision. He needs to know as much of what is going on as possible. He plays his part. Information of course is power. That is a well-known phrase. The Crown suggests that it was a calculated decision of the defendant to do what he had to do in going to the police station with that boy. Of course, he could rightly say—and I think he does say—that he would be damned if he did and damned if he did not blow that whistle. We say that is exactly right. We damn him because he had not blown the whistle. He did not blow the whistle on those earlier incidents. He did not tell the authorities at all when pupils were complaining of violence and of inappropriate behaviour. He was witnessing those unusual levels of violence that he reports about. He did not blow the whistle and the Crown does condemn him and damn him for that. There was no whistle blowing for at least two years.

When he does blow the whistle you might think he really had no choice. It was far from him acting alone, wasn't it? The matron was aware; the headmaster was aware; others would become aware. So the proverbial hits the fan. What does the defendant do? Well, the police are involved. Cadman is arrested. Cadman is released. The defendant claims he resigned pretty much straight after Cadman was released, almost as a protest at that. 21 st January 1989, he stated. When asked to clarify it by the judge he agreed. We know that, for example, to be nonsense. His resignation came just before half-term in February, as he put in his own book. It was not even the first time he had tried to resign. He was not just resigning on this issue. Perhaps he thought that staying around was dangerous.

There is an issue that is raised about pocket money and the letter that he responds to Mr. Cadman concerning the pocket money on 10th February. These things can be tricky. What is he going to do? Finally he decides that he will leave; best be away from there, out of sight and out of mind. That, of course, presents him with another dilemma. Andrew Hudson. What are we going to do about Andrew? With Alex Standish away of course he cannot exert anything like the same control on this young man in his charge. Who knows what he might say? It is OK when Andrew was giving a statement to the police in January. Mr. Standish was there as guardian. He has already had to tell Philip Cadman that Andrew must not be spoken to without him. As he puts in his own diary on 3rd February, "I threatened to withdraw the Ys and Andrew Hudson if Cadman questions them without me being present."

He wrote in a letter on the same date about Mr. Cadman "threatening to sack me on the spot if I removed my wards, X, Y and Andrew Hudson". He wrote in his own book, "I made that clear to Cadman in the office and also informed him that I would not have any of the three boys for whom I was acting as guardian questioned in my absence." Later, "Cadman however drew back from the brink and agreed that I could be present if he questioned those boys. Leaving the office I then produced a letter in which I stated that I would not attend the meeting and confirmed that he should not attempt to question my wards without me being in attendance." A great effort made by Alex Standish to ensure that Andrew wasn't asked—and indeed X and Y were not being asked—questions without him there.

When he leaves there are going to be all sorts of risks, aren't there? So a plan is perhaps hatched. A phone call is made to the parents in the Easter holidays to tell Keith of the defendant's fears for Andrew's safety; to give him advice to get Andrew out. As a friend, Keith takes that advice as good advice and he takes Andrew out of the school. That is problem solved. As X put it, "What kids were there in the summer were largely fifth formers." As we know there was one very notable exception from that—Andrew Hudson. X was back there. Z was back there. V was back there. All sorts of fifth formers were back there, yet the defendant claims he could not guarantee pupils' safety. Why weren't they taken out by him, by advice to their parents? Well, because they weren't sexually abused by him. Yes, there might have been some inappropriate hugging, some play fighting and the like, but that was unlikely, was it not, to get him into trouble. But masturbation and the unseemly use of the hair brush was a tricky issue and he had solved it. Andrew was away.

Of course, we know that events surrounding Crookham Court did not simply end with the defendant leaving the school. There were criminal trials. There were libels against the defendant. The defendant of course maintained some contact with Andrew. There were statements that he sought to obtain from Andrew for the High Court proceedings, but then not calling him into the witness box, despite you might think a very clear and detailed assertion in the police interview that he had called him; that you could get the transcripts; that he had been warned about perjury and still he said this. Is that another example of the defendant lying, blustering to the police in an effort to put them off?

After the school had closed down there were also invitations to Kent, to monitor the situation, to check that Andrew was still onside, to check that nothing was going to come out, to make sure that everything was OK. Then of course, after 1991 and the High Court proceedings had finished and the criminal proceedings had finished, no doubt things had cooled down significantly, what do you have after that? Well, really not much at all. Almost nothing. Andrew Hudson of course never lived with the defendant. Whilst others of his charges, of his wards, seemed to spend time living with him, there was no real need to maintain contact with Andrew Hudson. He was safe. He had got away with it.

We know that no matter what the delay, eventually he did complain. Eventually he made a very serious allegation, a number of allegations, against a teacher. Let us suppose then, just for a minute, that Andrew Hudson had some kind of malicious or selfish motive for saying that he had been sexually abused; that he had some reason for putting himself through questions from the social worker; some reason for being interviewed by the police at the police station after that first complaint; some reason for allowing himself to have to go through a video interview, to be asked intimate questions, and a second video interview that we did not show you but that he agreed that he'd had.

Suppose he had a motive for putting himself through that and the need to come to court two years later, talking about those embarrassing and those intimate details of himself as a boy and putting himself through that entire ordeal. Let us suppose he had something, just for a moment, to gain from suggesting that a teacher did that to him. Well, didn't he go to the right school to support that kind of allegation? Crookham Court was exposed on *That's Life!*. Teachers (plural) were arrested and prosecuted there. He has got the situation on a plate for him, hasn't he? He has a wealth of teachers to point at. Mr. Standish in the early part of his own book (on page 2) says, "The author does not question the guilt of the three men convicted in July 1990 although perhaps others should also have faced charges."

Andrew Hudson has the ideal school. There are all sorts of likely candidates to point the finger at: any one of a number. There is Philip Cadman, the principal, who we know in July 1990 was convicted of an offence of buggery and an offence of indecent assault and went to prison. We have [name redacted] who also was convicted in 1990, this time of four offences of buggery, seven offences of indecent assault (four of them committed at the school), and admitted twenty-four boys had been involved in indecent acts with him over his years. We have Dr. William Printer, the French teacher, also convicted of two offences of indecent assault and one offence of attempted buggery who, like his colleagues, went to prison. There was not going to be much difficulty convincing people that you had been touched by Dr. Printer, Mr. Cadman, [name redacted], or any convicted buggerer of boys, or paedophile. There might even be the advantage that one or more of them may well have passed away in the meantime. Mr. Cadman was particularly old and presumably has gone now. It is the easiest thing in the world, is it not, to say, if you have reason to, "Yes, I was sexually abused by Mr. Cadman. Did you know he has previously been convicted of just that sort of thing?" Or there was [name redacted] or Dr. Printer. Say all three if you like. They were all at it, weren't they, members of the jury?

But, no, who is the person that Andrew Hudson points out? Is it a dead teacher? Is it a convicted teacher? No, it is not; it is Alex Standish. It is his tutor, his apparent friend, and his family's friend. Of all the teachers that he could have chosen, why choose this one?

Andrew Hudson chose to tell police that Alex Standish had indecently assaulted him. There is only one logical, sensible explanation of why he did that. He did that because it is true. The defendant denies it. The defendant has given his account at great length and has been examined at great length. The documents that he produces have been examined. The inconsistencies—the falsities, I suggest—that he has told, the lies that he has told, have been examined. In the same way as you examine the evidence of Andrew Hudson, you will examine the evidence of Alex Standish. If you agree that he has told lies, you will want to consider why he has told lies. If you agree that he has told lies, in my submission that will support very much the Crown's case and support very much what Andrew Hudson has to say about this defendant.

What Andrew Hudson has to say about this defendant is that he abused him. No doubt it was a very difficult thing to say and to complain about; to drag back through those memories, to talk about those intimate things, and to shatter the relationship that Alex Standish had with other members of Andrew's family. Andrew's father, his mother, and his sister, Christine, regarded Alex Standish as a cherished member of the family. How does one go about seeking to destroy that? Does one do it lightly, or does one do it because one is compelled, because one is at breaking point, and because you are being destroyed, because one is worried that he is not the father that he wants to be and it is affecting him?

Andrew Hudson did not sit in his police interview or stand in the witness box in court and say, "That man is a monster with no redeeming features." He said, "That man did many good things. That man was often nice. Sometimes he was nasty."

Andrew Hudson said, "I thought he was being my friend." But what friend does that? What friend indeed.

In Aesop's fable of the North Wind and the Sun vying with each other to see which one would be able to get the man to take his coat off first, it is not the strength of the North Wind's gusts that blows it off him, but the gentle warm rays of the Sun.

This paedophile did not tear Andy's clothes off him. With words of kindness, helping him to pay off his debt, he got Andy naked. In the end, Andy simply undressed without being asked. It was with soft touching, not compulsion, that he brought Andy to orgasm.

By the time he had been stripped, masturbated, beaten, and raped, any feeling that he might be a victim was subsumed by his complicity in the silence that accompanied these crimes.

When the guilty verdict was delivered, Andy's body convulsed with sobs. His abuser had been sent down. He could try to get on with his life. He made a video describing what had happened to him, using graphic language and without shame, in the hope that others could follow.

Having met several men abused in childhood, it is clear to me that only when they are able to externalise the crime can they start to heal. While a man's erection is a sign that he is ready for sex, it is a physiological reaction that he has no control over. A male victim needs to understand that his body is reacting in the only way it can and that this readiness is not enjoyment.

For Andy, full disclosure to the world was his liberation.

THIRTEEN

Tougher than the wars I've fought in

Daniel (not his real name) was a soldier, invalided out on a pension and now running his own business. One of his contributions to the Crookham Court Facebook page spoke to me of a particular understanding of the plight of the adults abused in childhood. The conversation was about what should be done with the building. It had been sitting empty for several years and was succumbing to nature. Daniel's contribution was nothing if not forthright. He wanted it bulldozed. The building deserved it.

Another contributor responded that it was not the building that had caused any bad memories for people and that for many the memories were wonderful.

Daniel's reply was instant and to the effect that the previous writer could not have been there when children's innocence was being stolen and that the building stood like a monument to the crimes that had happened within it.

I replied: "There are powerful emotions coming across, Daniel. Sometimes it takes ages to come to a realisation. Call me."

Daniel told me he was fine, but that he had scars. Scars. I knew then that whatever they were, they were deep.

"Take your time. You won't forget, but you can put things into perspective from an adult's point-of-view now. None of the children should have been in that situation; none of them should feel guilty. The guilt rests in those who were in charge of them."

Daniel had, indeed, been touched. He did not want to take anything any further.

"Daniel, I won't ask you to do anything. Yes, Andy was brave. He was also at the end of his tether. He needed to unburden. And you are doing this, too. Take it at your own pace. Tell me what you want when you want to tell me. I won't tell anyone anything unless you want it said. What you are telling me is between us."

He did not tell his father at the time and he still had not told him twenty-five years later. He would not have understood. The other boys did, though. Daniel was threatened and beaten as a warning to say nothing to anyone.

"I can understand how the young Daniel in 1989 wanted to get away from it all. The mature Daniel is able to be objective. Whatever you decide, I'm with you."

Some time after this exchange I saw Daniel was online and contacted him via Google video. He was in Australia. I would have recognised him in the street. His London accent remained, though with Australian intonation, his voice rising at the end of the sentence as if to make a statement a question.

He was a dark-haired, chisel-featured man of forty, his shoulder muscles powerful under his white shirt. We cut to the chase after a few minutes' small talk.

He told me how he had served in war zones in the army, how he had been in battle—and how he had never been as frightened in these theatres of war as he had been at Crookham Court School. "I knew what he wanted, [name redacted]. He never penetrated me, but, you know. And he was the one I ran to after [name redacted] tried it on with me. I went to tell him. I trusted him. And I ran from him. And these boys, his special boys, they went after me. They beat me."

"They knew he'd tried it on with you and you weren't having it and this was their way of punishing you?"

"Or their way of telling me not to say anything. They knew and they were out to protect him."

Boys were after him, beating him, attacking him for not having given in to a paedophile. They were protecting a paedophile. It was this madness that Daniel could not overcome.

Daniel never did make a complaint. The teacher's praetorian guard and what he had narrowly escaped from at the hands of two teachers so terrified him from a distance of twenty-five years and the other side of the world, that he did not take it further and I did not push him into doing so. The loyalty of boys of seventeen to a paedophile teacher would stretch to perjury in the years that followed. Daniel fell silent; his issues unresolved; his parents, wife, and family ignorant.

Alan Young (not his real name) was also a contributor to the Facebook page. By private message, I asked him, "Were you touched?"

His reply alluded to smelling [name redacted]'s breath. He told me he went blank from that point and that for years he had tried not to remember. It was he who had been chosen to be Cadman's note-taker. He had been given a notebook and, if anyone did anything wrong, he had to note it down. Then, once or twice a week, he had to stay behind and go through the book with him. He would sit at his desk and he, the boy, would have to stand beside him. Then the abuse took place. He told me that when it came out on *That's Life!* in 1989, he had been asked by his parents if anything had happened to him and he had lied that it had not.

This was the first time that he had spoken about these events.

"And now you have spoken about it. And what may have happened to you, happened to other children. Maybe you lied to your mum and dad to protect them. As you tell me that you lied to them that you were OK, I assume you were not OK. It's your decision what to do. I will support you whatever you decide."

His reply was that he had young children and that he needed time to think about the implications of disclosing.

"You said what you said because you trust me. And because you needed to say it. I respect you totally for this. It took Andy more than twenty years. When he disclosed, he told me everyone around him was 100 per cent supportive. And that he felt so much better. We'll take this at your pace. There's no shame in any of it. Nor guilt. What Andy found difficult was that his body responded to the abuse. It would. Boys' bodies do. It doesn't mean they are complicit. He also lied about it. He was consumed by shame and guilt. He now knows that he need not have been. May I tell Andy? You can trust him just as you can trust me.'

That was agreed.

"You're the one in charge. I shall mention it to Andy. That's all. You're in safe hands. You're with people who understand and can go forward with you if that's where you want to go."

I later wrote:

> "Andy now knows. It's an odd feeling for you because you've bottled it up for decades. Now you can take it out, look at it and say to yourself, 'Hey, this should never have happened to me. The man who did this was wrong. He needs to be brought to justice.' You will then start to feel liberated. What happened was a crime and you're the innocent victim. Everyone will understand why you left it so long. Andy's dad (who knows nothing about you at all—no one does) will be happy to liaise with other mums and dads if wanted."

I was thanked for not judging him.

"No one will judge you because you did nothing wrong. You lied to protect."

He told me he felt better for having told someone.

Later, I wrote, "It seems [name redacted] had yet another victim—apart from you. I assume you were one."

He told me he had been.

"Then you know what you should do."

Alan never did get his head around these events. Some weeks after these exchanges, he blanked me from Facebook and I did not hear from him again. A boy in his year group contacted me separately and confirmed that he, too, had suspected Alan was being abused. Alan's abuser remains at liberty and uncontactable. His family has, I am sure, no idea what happened to him all those years ago.

[Name redacted] was a huge man. Children have spoken of their fear of his size, his larger-than-life presence, and his booming voice. He taught in his graduate gown which he swirled around him and, for the school photograph, he appeared in his full red regalia and cap. The grown-ups told him this looked ludicrously incongruous. No child dared utter a word. We saw a man of such self-importance, he was ridiculous. What has come across from the children who have spoken to me about him is that their perception was quite different. They saw him towering above them and feared him. I had no idea of the power he wielded. With colleagues, he was almost silent and generally absent from the staff common room. I never uttered a complete sentence to him, let alone had a conversation.

Sexual abuse is a secret crime whose victims go to great lengths to cover it up, as do their abusers. Knowing now, as we do, that it can happen and that if it happens it is likely to be well-disguised, at least sensitises us to the possibility. Before the Crookham Court exposé, few seriously imagined that professional teachers were capable of such base actions. My young sons have met more abusers and their victims than most children their age. I talk to them openly about the crime of abuse and the various forms it takes. "Your body is your own and it's private," I tell them. "It's up to you whom you let touch it. If there is something you don't want, say 'no'."

"And then tell you so you can get them arrested, Daddy?"

"Yes. That's the way I do things."

FOURTEEN

Abusive language and behaviour become the norm

It was a casual remark from Andy in 2012 (personal conversation) that started me thinking.

"Oh, he was OK as a teacher. He was nice."

"Was he, Andy? He was living with one of the boys at the time, wasn't he?"

"Oh, yes. I'd forgotten that."

Andy had "forgotten" that small fact. A fact that would in any normal establishment have got the man sacked at least, if not arrested. At Crookham Court, he was given a senior position. What was in Andy's head that made him "forget", that enabled him to see as normal a situation that would have been incredible anywhere else? What keeps on happening becomes its own "normality". It could only be that he had, at a formative age, been in a world in which the normal societal mores were upside down; where there was no moral guidance; no moral leadership. How do people react when the normal course of events is turned upside down? When this first happened in 1977, the term Cadman banned the parents and Christmas, there was a clear desire for "business as usual". Something was very wrong and it masked the abuse that lay behind it, but such was the desire for normality that the chaos was incorporated into it. While the nonsense continued, the focus was on the minutiae of the nonsense, not the havoc it caused. All the time abuse on a widening scale became rife. For the abused children, abuse became normal. Andy and other boys who have spoken to me eventually stripped naked as a matter of course without being told to. This is what they had been told to do by those in authority, this is what had become expected of them and they complied.

And it was not just Andy who came to see what was unacceptable as the norm. This had been normality for scores of boys in those formative years when an awareness of a benign authority is vital, when their perception of the adult world is being shaped. My feeling is that the boys who were in that school from September 1977 until July 1989 could not take for granted that the place they were in was constructed to develop and encourage them as people; to cultivate, foster, or even simply to protect them, and that these children may have been damaged in some way by being part of the developing chaos. In such an upside-down culture where anything was permitted and no overarching authority seemed to care, small events that would have led to an investigation in another school just continued unchecked.

A conversation on Facebook involving several of those at the school after 1977 indicated just how insensitive at best, and brutal at worst, they had become. They also seem to have forgotten much of the English I tried to teach them. It started with a factual posting from me:

> "If you have been a witness to any events involving others or yourself at Crookham Court, please contact Charles at crd@verisona.com or contact me. He is pursuing the company to compensate those affected. It's important that everyone who has any information at all reveals it so that those who have been affected achieve the compensation they deserve."

One of the former pupils, now a middle-aged man, asked if compensation extended to damage inflicted by hard lavatory paper.

Andy wrote: "sorry J, you may laugh but it is no laughing matter and find it very offensive you can joke about other peoples misery".

His response was to say that's what happens when the same Facebook page is used for serious matters and sharing a joke and that if Andy couldn't take it, he would leave the page.

Andy wrote: "no dont leave, we are all pissed off … i have tried to put good memories on this page too but unfortunately it did happen and nothing can be done about it …"

Another former pupil jumped in to ask that all the many good times be remembered.

I wrote: "Whether it's serious or trivial, it's all to do with managing the appropriateness of the response. Many TV programmes combine the two. Generally adults can deal with this."

I should not have interceded.

Yet another old boy responded to take me to task for not having spotted earlier what Cadman was up to and not having pulled out when I thought he was unsuitable. He also told Andy he had a victim mentality, that Cadman had a distinguished war record and that he had enjoyed his time at the school. He described me as liberal and intolerant of alternative views.

Andy wrote: "alternative view or ignorant????"

I wrote: "Let me make it clear that there were no disclosures, allegations or suspicions of abuse relating to Cadman before 1989. What was disturbing was his inability to be in charge of children. His ability to be in charge of children was vested in him by the relevant authorities who were informed frequently of these shortcomings. In those days, social services and other bodies had no right of entry. The Children Act was altered in

1989 as it passed through Parliament in the light of the events at Crookham. No individual action other than the action that was taken could have been taken against him in the 1980s or before."

Andy wrote: "ian has said often enough, he never suspected abuse, what he is trying to gather was evidence to say cadman was a crap teacher and wasnt capable of looking after boys ie a proper principal … we all wish the world wasnt softer but it has and i say for the better … thousands of ex veterans from world war 1 and 2 had many problems and were told to just man up and couldnt … the needed care not being told that and this continues to this day … i have many friends who have seen combat in both gulf wars and many tours of iraq and afghanistan and clocked up more combat hours than world war vets … i suppose they should just man up as well then … i hope you dont have to be in the position of seeing your best friend blown to bits in front of your eyes or using the example watching your best friend starve to death or get beaten to death by the japs … i could guess why your neighbor said nothing … because of attitudes like yours … you and your attitude are quite stuck in the past … and should be like the dinosaurs … extinct!"

The reply, in essence, although the expressions used were colourful, was that Crookham Court was typical of boarding schools.

Andy wrote: "you are just so stuck in the mud and will never listen to others … lets just agree to disagree … you are uncaring smug git who has had such a good life and thinks that if people moan they are wimps … ok … i for one will be glad when this type of attitude is gone … its like thatcher … unneeded and we wonder why this country is up shit creek … cause of attitudes like yours … stuff you lot i am ok … i hope we never met as you come across as one hell of a selfish smug prick … sorry just MY opinion of you … ."

The response was that just as he had saved, used his resources, and got on in life, so should Andy—and that he should control his anger.

Andy wrote: "anger management … no you need to shove your head up your arse and learn some compassion … i hope to god we never meet … and as for running down crookham … no we just want people to recognize what happened and not deny it or come up with smug comments like man up and get on with it … they are uncalled for and unwanted … a bit like yourself really … no go away and be uncaring elsewhere you toffy nose prick … ."

The reply to this was that the Crookham Court case was trial by TV.

Andy wrote: "would you rather people forgot the abuse? People that forget the mistakes are gonna let it happen again and again! As for whining, no I am not just getting fed up of attitudes like yours—its because of attitudes like yours that victims are scared to come forward! As for violence … at what point did I offer you out! Without lowering myself to your level, you sir aren't worth the steam of my piss, now please take your dinosaur attitude and shove up your bloated fat arse, if there is room up there along side your rather fat head."

Another correspondent joined in to say that Andy should "grow some" and that he could not understand why Andy had not hit the man.

Andy wrote: "dont you think i have asked myself this question … i was scared is the only answer … he was a big bloke compared to me as a 14 year old boy … i have grown a set … its called reporting him and then having to stand up in court and get cross examined … not for the faint hearted … i just get pissed off when people say just grow a set and man up and move on … its been proven that attitude hasnt and doesnt work … it has left me with many unseen problems … but i fight them every day … something that is harder than just growing a set … as for the way you asked … why do it any other way … lol … direct and to the point … ."

Another respondent sensibly suggested that they should talk about other things on the page.

I gave them the chance to do this, creating the "Survivors of Crookham Court (and their friends)" page. Henceforward, those who did not want to know what had happened did not have to.

So, middle-aged men in their forties resorted to shouting rude words at each other in cyberspace. Middle-aged men with children who had no idea what those abused in childhood have endured and were unwilling to let them express their feelings. And some of these middle-aged men were themselves abused. One them—I shall call him Nathaniel (not his real name)—wrote in a private message how the events at Crookham had made him the man he is today and he did not regret them; that he lost trust in people; that he destroyed everything around him; that his life had been devastated, but that he had dealt with his demons and was now a stronger person.

On the page, Nathaniel wrote how his memories of Crookham were only happy ones. What he experienced became the norm.

Happy memories was the theme of the "official" Old Crookhamians group. They comprised only boys who attended between the school's founding in 1961 and 1966. Anyone after 1966 would not receive an acknowledgement if they tried to join. They would also not accept that Cotton was anything other than a great headmaster. Whatever he was and did became the norm of headmastership.

Life at Crookham Court in the 1960s was summed up by an old boy of that time (email, 14 October 2013): "He [Cotton] was sometimes hard on us and we did have the cane for fooling around which today would have been considered trivial. The abuse we suffered at Crookham was more like a boot camp insomuch that we were forced to go into the outdoor swimming pool with the water being 58 degrees f, runs around the air base at 6.30am in the morning during the midst of winter, no heating in the dorms with Mr. Cotton keeping the windows wide open. I can remember one boy with snow on his bed during the winter of 1962/63. All of this of course toughened us up and we were very fit having to perform sports activities most days. We were told by Roy Cotton in the summer of 1966 that he had decided not to remain at Crookham as he was entering the Church."

And like most boys, he believed what he was told. After writing to me, however, he contacted another old boy who was not so forthcoming about the joys of life as a pupil at the 1960s Crookham Court (email, 14 October 2013):

> "Whilst it is a matter for the record that Roy had a conviction for a minor offence which occurred in the 1950's, and which the Church and his employers deemed a 'misunderstanding', I can say with absolute certainty that during his time at Crookham Court, there was never a single complaint against him. On the contrary, he was highly regarded and much admired by both staff and pupils, and departed the school with full honours. Many of his ex-pupils continued to stay in touch with him for many years after his departure. Whilst I am aware of certain allegations made against him since he left Crookham, in some cases by attention-seeking individuals, he was never charged with any offence, and is not able to defend himself against these allegations. I have to ask, therefore, what your motive can be in digging over this information, given that you never had any direct connection with him, are not party to the allegations, and do not represent a law enforcement agency. Your interest would appear to be prurient. Your enquiries are deeply disturbing, and those of us who knew and remember Roy, would rather that you let this matter be. You should be aware that old boys

from the 1960's have already used the threat of a law suit to warn off a BBC journalist who was similarly disposed."

The original writer told me he had reported me to the "spokesperson" for the old boys association. (Email, 15 October 2013):

> "We feel as an Old Boys group very upset at your continual allegations concerning Roy Cotton. As [name redacted] rightly pointed out, nothing untoward happened with Roy Cotton during his time at Crookham. He is not here to defend himself and we feel you should let the matter rest as no evidence is forthcoming during his Crookham Court years. You must try to differentiate between sexual abuse and punishments that were handed down to us over 50 years ago which today may be considered a form of non sexual abuse all those years ago. In those days the word abuse was never mentioned and many private and public schools handed out punishments of a similar nature. As boys we accepted this form of strict discipline. We felt it was part of our upbringing Ian. What you probably don't know is that some of the boys' fathers had served in the armed forces and wanted their sons to be disciplined in the same way. I would strongly recommend that you let the matter rest now Ian as nothing can be gained and will certainly never be proved. [Name redacted] threatened a BBC journalist with legal action so this is worth taking on board. I am still happy to meet one and all at any future reunions and I certainly will bear no malice towards you. I hope this clearly explains my position and please remember that the Old Boys had the most utmost respect for Roy."

Such was the atmosphere of the school at that time and the recollected feelings of loyalty to a man who had, indeed, been convicted of a crime against a boy and for whose subsequent abusive behaviour the Church of England has apologised, accepting that he should never have been ordained, that in the face of a recorded criminal conviction, an apology from the Church of England and the recorded experiences of many of his victims, there was no acceptance of the truth of any of this.

An old boy wrote to me (email, 14 October 2013):

> "I hope the Crookham re-development is well under way. The Old Boys are hoping when the main House is finished that we can be allowed to erect a plaque in honour of the past Old Boys and staff at the school."

The ties that bind the "official" Old Crookhamians group ensure that the affection its members have for their alma mater transcend any documented evidence that all was not well with the leadership of the establishment they love. I wondered what made this group "official" without an office to confer this title. They had a leader, a spokesman, and a stated aim to revere the school they attended, excluding anyone who was there after their time, after Cotton left.

For them, their schooldays were the best days. They have the ability to deal with any negatives simply by denying them. This triumph of belief over fact is so overwhelming that, although it flies in the face of evidence, it may as well be true and for them Crookham Court School between 1961 and 1966 was a great place to grow up and to be a pupil.

FIFTEEN

Keeping a secret

Keith Cavendish-Coulson came to Crookham Court in the autumn of 1971 to teach French. He was a tall, willowy thirty year old with wavy blond hair, a billowing gown, colourful clothes, a cut-glass public school accent, and a penchant for long words. In the fullness of time, forty years later, it came out that he was the son of a post office worker whose old school tie was from a comprehensive in Stockport. The double-barrelled name was an invention. "Cavendish" had been added along the way.

At one of our first meetings, he told me he had come straight from prison for fraud.

"Now why on earth would he tell me this?" I wondered. "And what should I do with this information?"

As I discovered later, it's a human trait to side with the underdog, to protect the person involved in rule-breaking, and to keep a secret that has been vouchsafed to you. I had, in effect, become complicit in his wrongdoing right from the start. If I told his employer, it was breaking a confidence. He would likely be sacked. It was a confidence I had not wanted, nor felt I had earned, but it had been given to me as a trust, and to break it would be a breach of faith in some odd way. It was not incumbent on me to tell anyone and I did not, but from that moment I felt privy to something that was not quite right. In fact, I was protecting an abuser.

Slowly, he imparted more information to me. "I corrupted a prison visitor there," he told me. He did not specify the gender of the visitor, but I assumed it was a male. He told me how to spot an ex-con. "If anyone tells you they can do bookbinding, it's a cert they've been inside." He had put this down as a skill on his CV and maybe blamed his employer for not spotting this crucial giveaway. "I met a forger in the Scrubs," he told me. "He did my references."

I was getting too much information. I avoided him.

"Just been crinkling," he commented when a boy left his room after a private French lesson. When that boy left the school, Keith Cavendish-Coulson—KCC as he was known—wrote a note which he gave me. "Que je suis desolé(e)." All the clues were there and still I did nothing. I had no idea what to do. I was in my early twenties and liked to think the best of people. The man was testing my limits. He told me there were code words for finding out if someone was interested in men, such as, "Is he by any chance interested in music?"; "Is he at all musical?"; and the ultimate, "Might he be a professional musician?" I was intrigued by the novelty of it all, but I found I believed nothing he said. I came to disbelieve he had been in prison. It was all too extreme. "My mother drives this yellow thing that bangs about. It begins with a 'L'." "Lamborghini?" I ventured. "That's it!"

It was easy to dismiss his stories as inventions. As long as I just listened and humoured him, that is all they were—stories. Unreal stories. As I realised later, I was being groomed.

The boys enjoyed his lessons; the other teachers found him convivial; I kept my distance. I assumed he was a Walter Mitty and essentially harmless. This was the general feeling.

KCC was a genial and erudite man with a line in nonce-words. "Lunchingtons," he would observe when the gong for mealtimes was sounded. "… ingtons" was a suffix he would give many words. It gave them a cosy sound. Later he would put a "word for today" on his telephone answering machine. His record player was a gramophone and his radio a wireless. He eschewed modernisms and was a typical young fogey. He loved electrical apparatus, though, and had hooks installed on a beam that ran across the ceiling of his tiny bedsit in the school on which he would hang small appliances such as headphones and transistor radios. They looked like trophies and, indeed, they were.

During the Easter hols (as I write KCCesque-words are uppermost in my mind), an old friend of Keith's came to the school to visit him. Keith was not there. He told me about it later. "He went in and was wandering around when he bumped into the Commander. He told him he was looking for me and that we were old friends. The Commander asked him how he knew me and he told him we were in prison together."

Ever keen to see the best in people, Robert Smithwick allowed him to stay on as a teacher. I was relieved that the secret was out.

At the start of the first term of his second year, he was brought back to the school from one of his shopping expeditions in the back of a police car, having been arrested for shoplifting. His trophies were taken away as evidence and he was convicted on multiple counts. Robert's toleration reached its end and KCC departed Crookham Court for pastures new. It seemed he was given a chance to start afresh and he was appointed to a post at Terra Nova in Cheshire, a prep school. If his record preceded him, it was not held against him.

In fact, Keith Cavendish-Coulson had quite a record before he came to Crookham Court, with a conviction from 1964 for importuning and for theft in 1969, both offences resulting in fines. He had, indeed, been to prison and in 1970 he pleaded guilty to various offences of fraud, uttering forged cheques, and obtaining property by deception, with a large number of matters taken into consideration. The offences were committed with two others. He would adopt the names of peers of the realm typed onto cheques in order to obtain property from various retail outlets. He received a sentence of two and a half years' imprisonment. For the shoplifting in Newbury in 1973, he was sentenced to a period of probation for three years.

KCC's connection with Crookham Court paused for a couple of decades, but he would return and it was his return that would lead to his downfall.

As Oscar Wilde might have remarked: "To have one abusive French teacher may be regarded as a misfortune; to have two looks like carelessness."

When Cavendish-Coulson left Crookham Court via Newbury Magistrates Court, he was replaced by a chubby, dark-haired young French teacher. He had interesting letters after his name that I had not seen before. They appeared at top of every note he wrote, preprinted in red ink. He was Benedict Greville, PhD (Cand) which, glanced at quickly, gave the impression that he had a doctorate from Cambridge. In fact "Cand" stood for "candidate". He was planning to take the exam. Greville's customary pose was to stand with his fingertips together speaking in a quietly authoritative voice as if giving a papal edict ex cathedra. From a distance, his head looked tonsured and, both in bearing and in tone, he oozed religiosity. He eschewed the company of most staff members and stayed for a year or two, developing a coterie of boys to whom, we assumed, he pontificated and discussed doctrinal matters. He made it clear to them he disliked me in particular. "He calls you 'Digger', sir," one of them told me. I wondered if he thought I was trying to dig up information on him. I had little chance to do so before one of his acolytes decided he had seen enough of Greville's caressing of a dark-haired, brown-eyed fourteen-year-old boy and complained to the Commander. Greville made a tearful departure the same day. "He'll never teach again," the boy was assured, probably because he would not receive a reference from Crookham Court. As his activities were not reported to any authority, the lack of a reference would have been a minor and surmountable inconvenience.

SIXTEEN

Google will find you out

In the years that followed his departure, KCC sent me brief notes from Terra Nova and then from wherever he was at the time, sometimes schools, sometimes large country houses in Europe and America. He was into private tutoring and contact was lost. In the mid-'90s I was told he was at Crookham Court. A friend told me KCC had told him that his mother had said he should befriend Cadman in his hour of need on his release from prison. He became Cadman's right-hand man, working for him in exchange for accommodation. In 1997 he showed me round the school. It was my first visit there since it closed in 1989. The rooms had become bedsits, rented out "to those on housing benefit", he told me. "Philip likes to go round with a bunch of keys." KCC seemed to enjoy this, too. It was a role reversal from their prison days. I felt uneasy inside the building and glimpsed Cadman in there. It was another ten years before I came near it again.

When Cadman died in 2007, I again made contact with KCC who was the closest I could find to anyone in charge and asked him if my six-year-old sons could run around in the jungle that the grounds had become. They loved romping in the head-high vegetation and flew their remote-controlled helicopters away from trees in the middle of what had been the croquet lawn.

KCC invited us inside and we saw his room. It was the surgery the matron had used, piled high with what looked like the contents of charity shops and had, indeed, been sourced from there. "Miss Havisham" is what a friend called him when I showed her round the crumbling wreckage of the building. The tenants had departed. The inheritors were planning to redevelop their inheritance. KCC was their watchdog. He referred to them by their first names and told me some of the details of their plans. I asked him if he could arrange for the old boys to be allowed to see the school and he passed on the request. I mentioned on the Crookham Court Facebook page that Keith Cavendish-Coulson was allowing his garden to be used for the reunion.

The annual get-together happened in June and, although the old boys spent most of their time at the local pub—which many knew well from illicit visits during their schooldays—and were not allowed in the building, they were quite happy to break in and see the decay for themselves. KCC moved out of the school when it became unsafe and took up residence in what had been the headmaster's lodge at the end of the drive. He would still answer the phone "Crookham House", never Crookham Court, and although he allowed the old boys to use his lawn, he remained inside on these annual occasions and was seen by no one. I thought it odd at the time. Now I realise that he had no idea who was coming to these gatherings and might have been recognised by someone who would have good reason to remember him. Over the years, although our visits were infrequent, he came to know my sons. He taught them how to eat a banana with a spoon, how to tie a tie properly, let them play his piano, and gave them books.

My sons thought KCC was a loner. I was not so sure. He told me he had become a visitor to the secure unit across the road and how he had befriended inter alia an Old Etonian who had murdered his mother. "Charming and quite bonkers," he said. The lodge was filled with mementoes of his teaching days, photos of boys he had taught and big houses he had tutored in. He loved to mention famous schools whose pupils he had tutored and in 2011, he was able to mention a well-known name. He showed me a letter from a Government minister, to whom he had written, commiserating with him on his appearance at the Leveson Inquiry, and whose reply recalled his time as KCC's pupil.

During the Standish trial, I asked him for information about the layout of the school, but on a second enquiry, he told me he had destroyed all the school records. Whether he had or not, I had no idea, but I sensed he did not welcome my enquiries. The Crookham Court Facebook page was well-established by then and I mentioned that Keith Cavendish-Coulson had destroyed the records and that I had no idea why. When I asked him later why he had done this, he was quite open in telling me this was on the instruction of the owners. I put this on the Facebook page, too. He called me the "Witchfinder General" behind my back and disapproved of my hostility towards Cadman and all he represented. I told him I knew his laissez-faire attitude towards the man and I never broached this subject with him. Our conversations were always guarded. He was the only link I had with the school. I imagined the family knew all about my hostility towards their relative. The only contact I had with their local agent had been when I asked if a victim of abuse at the school could revisit the scene of the crime. I was turned down flat.

For all his interest in electronic gadgetry, KCC told me he did not possess a computer or use the internet. The internet contained two or three mentions of his name on the Facebook pages and one from the local newspaper from twenty years before quoting his comment about supposed UFO sightings at the time. This is all a Google search would reveal. Few though they were, these mentions were to prove to be his undoing.

As the children's wish to romp diminished, our visits to Crookham Court School and therefore to KCC dwindled. They ended completely in November 2012 when I received a private message on Facebook via the Survivors of Crookham Court page. The writer had found the name he had been looking for in the brief mention I made that Keith Cavendish-Coulson had destroyed the Crookham Court records. He is happy that I use his real name.

> 08.11.12
>
> I am not sure if you can be of assistance but whilst searching the name Keith Cavendish-Coulson I was directed to the crookham court Facebook page which mentions his name in relation to the school. I am attempting to find out if this is the same gentleman whom was a teacher at Terra Nova a prep school in Cheshire. This would have been in about 1973/75. Hope you can be of assistance.
>
> Regards
>
> Rob Harding

I replied the same day: "He's the same one."

> 08.11.12
>
> Ian
>
> Thank you for your reply. I take it that he is still alive? This is somewhat difficult for me but certain memories seem to be increasingly haunting me in relation to my time at that school despite my 50th birthday next week. I just wanted some information especially given what occurred at Crookham.
>
> Best regards
>
> 09.11.12
>
> Oh yes, he's still alive.
>
> I am aware of several aspects of KCC.

You're welcome to call me, if it would help. My mobile is 07 …

Ian

09.11.12

Thanks for the reply. I will give you a call. However, I live in Australia so will have to make sure I call at an appropriate time. What would be a good time for you uk time? I am often back in the uk to visit family and so do appreciate your assistance with this.

Best regards

09.11.12

KCC "left" Crookham Court in 1973 and went to Terra Nova. There were events before and during his time at CC. He returned when Cadman was released from prison and functioned as his, shall we say, assistant. When he died, Cadman's relatives kept him on. He lives in a house down the drive from the main building.

As you use the word "haunted", I have an idea what you want to talk about. Please feel you can talk frankly and in confidence.

Best.

Ian

09.11.12

This is difficult. It is something that I have not discussed with anyone for 37 years. It is something I have managed to keep in the deeper recesses of my mind for all this time but in recent years those events that occurred at

Terra Nova seem to have become increasingly prominent. 2 years ago I visited TN with my daughter who is now 12: Today the school seems a really happy nurturing environment and my daughter loved being shown around by a couple of the girls she wanted to start boarding there!! For myself it was hard but I managed to internalise any emotions as I have done for so many years.

KCC sexually abused a number of boys myself included during his time at TN. Apparently he was caught by the Headmaster at the time a Mr. Best (somewhat oxymoronic name) and just left as far as I understand. The whole episode was swept under the carpet to clearly avoid any adverse publicity for the school. I never made mention of any of this as my parents were living overseas and there was a huge element of shame and guilt. If nothing else the whole episode instilled in myself a deep reticence and an utter distrust of those in positions of power. My survival mechanism after this was predominantly through violence. I found that to deal with the shame as well as the endemic bullying I would fight. I never bullied anyone and always looked after the downtrodden but certainly I can see my behaviour as a teenager and young man as stemming from these events. Even being on the other side of the world has not diminished these events although today I am more at peace with the world in general.

However, I am truly blessed with 2 wonderful children and a great family who know nothing of these events which is how I wish it to remain. What is hard to reconcile now is why these events have become so prominent in my thoughts and why I starting searching. What seems to beggar belief is how TN was more interested in maintaining its reputation than ensuring further crimes were not committed at the next institution.

Best

10.11.12

Thank you for your trust. I know from having met abused children how hard it is to confront these emotions.

Your school distanced itself from the events because it could. It is less easy now as the climate has changed, but it still happens. These people continue to abuse. The climate may have changed, but human nature has not. The only way to stop them is to put them in prison. There will continue to be abusers in positions of authority for as long as they are able to transfer the guilt and shame that you mention onto their victims. This is what Andy Hudson had to confront. He couldn't stand the nightmares. He told me. He told his family. He told the police. He has no regrets whatsoever. When we analysed everything that happened to him, his abuser's modus operandi became clear and he was able to see how he had been duped. What gave him terrible problems was the fact that when he was abused, he had an erection. He now knows that it wasn't because he was enjoying it, but because it's a physiological reaction in males.

You have identified the damage it has done to you. There will have been damage to all the boys who were abused before, during and after TN. Currently, KCC is a part-time visitor of vulnerable people in a psychiatric hospital and has had, and may still have, private pupils at his home. You see my dilemma. I have been pretty sure about him, but no one has made a complaint.

I think there is a reason for the events of your childhood to surface now. What would you say if your own children were to say to you in years to come, "I was abused, Daddy, but I didn't tell you because I was ashamed"? You can hear yourself saying, "I wish you had told me. There's no need to be ashamed." Or, indeed, if they said, "I thought you wouldn't understand" or "I thought you'd be angry."

The fact is that an abuser makes his victim complicit in the secrecy of the crime. This complicity makes the abused feel the guilt that should be exclusively the preserve of the abuser.

"All that is necessary for the triumph of evil is that good men do nothing," as Edmund Burke said. Since Andy put a stop to Standish, other men have told me they, too, suffered, but remained silent. As Andy did the job, they remain silent. You say your "family know nothing of these events which is how I wish it to remain". What has happened, though, is that you have changed the status quo. You have disclosed. You did so because you knew you had to. And I imagine you feel better for having done so.

But you now have to consider all the other people involved—the other boys at TN and elsewhere and the vulnerable people your abuser works with.

You can do nothing. You will, however, know that you had the power to stop an abuser and chose to let him continue.

Or you can do something. You can tell your family that you are one of the many, many children who had their childhood taken from them; who were put in a situation they should never have been put in; who did not know how to deal with the crime committed on them or the criminals who did it; who sought wrongly to protect those they loved from sharing the burden, but who now realise that love and trust are what is important and that, with love and trust, what was wrong can be put right.

And you were and are not guilty. You never were—and you are not now.

None of this is easy for me to write. I look at my sons. They loved to play in the jungle that was the grounds of Crookham Court School and to get there, we had to go via KCC. They know him. I feel for what you have suffered and for the memories that haunt you. My boys will be starting public school very soon. I want them to grow up in a society in which, if anything happens to a child, he tells a trusted adult, he is believed and the abuser is taken out of society. I'm sure you wish this, too. You have it in your power to help create this society. It's starting to be like this in this country. In Andy's case, his word was believed. This is increasingly the case.

I hope for the sake of your children and mine and for all children everywhere that you will trust in your family's love for you and let me take this one step further.

If you want to tell me first what happened to you, as Andy did, please go ahead. My boys are in school all today. Whatever you decide, I shall be here for you and you can tell me what needs to be told.

Best.

Ian

11.11.12

Ian

Thank you for your response. It may sound like a delaying tactic and it may well be but currently my mother has been taken into hospital back in the uk, she is 85 and so the family focus is on her well being. I have a sister in London who has travelled up to be with her but as you can understand my being so far away I do not wish to burden the family at this juncture.

However, the fact that he may still be abusing strikes a very poignant point and one that I need to consider very seriously.

Best

11.11.12

Good morning/evening. Thanks for your reply.

You are self-aware. You know that there will never be a good time to deal with the situation that KCC has created for both of us.

Andy was very fragile when he disclosed to me. He needed my support—which he got and always will have—but he also needed to have his family's support to get through this and other traumas in his life. I may be quite wrong, but you don't strike me as fragile. Apprehensive of the enormity of what you can do, certainly, but not fearful for your own well-being.

I also imagine you don't feel the need to seek your family's permission to expose an abuser.

That said, why don't you and I take this forward? These things take time. The wheels of the police and the Crown Prosecution Service grind slowly and the time when you feel it's right to let your family know may be a while away.

Given that this man still tutors children (see the attached which gives an idea about his standards of behaviour) and has access to very vulnerable people in a secure facility across the road from where he lives at Crookham Court School, I really think that doing nothing is not an option.

But I can do nothing without you.

Best.

Ian

11.11.12

This all seems somewhat bizarre in many respects. One minute I am googling KCC, finding the Crookham court information then next minute disclosing to you events which occurred all those years ago. However, given he has access to young children to this day I do feel compelled to act. The question being in what manner given the logistics of living 12000 miles away? So where to from here?

Best

12.11.12

Thanks.

Yes, it's absolutely the right thing to do. One way forward is for me to present our exchange of e-mails to my contact at Thames Valley Police, A. She was in charge of Andy's case. She has also met KCC, of course, when she was gathering documents at Crookham Court.

A better way forward is for me to give you her e-mail address and that you tell her that you and others were sexually abused by KCC when you were at TN. In that case, I'll send her an e-mail telling her that you found KCC through the CC FB page and explain our connection. She and I spoke at the trial about other victims. We were sure others would come forward.

So just choose one of the above and then the wheels will be set in motion.

I'll be off to bed soon, so I'll act on what you decide in the morning.

Best.

Ian

12.11.12

Ian

Send me her e-mail address I will contact her

Best

12.11.12

Hello again.

I have sent an e-mail to A and also spoken to her. She is very interested in the case. She is at Reading Crown Court at the moment, but will read the e-mail when she's back. She has told me the procedure. She will become involved, but, although KCC is now resident in Newbury, as the crime was committed in Cheshire, Cheshire Police need to be the first port-of-call.

As ever.

Ian

12.11.12

Ian

Thanks for the information. I will compile an e-mail to the Cheshire police soonest. I need to try to verify dates and years as at this stage those details are somewhat hazy. One thing I did mean to ask was how you fit into all this as I am not that well versed with the Crookham court case and so feel the need to fill in some more background details as I proceed which I am sure you would think the prudent thing to do.

Best

15.11.12

Just to say that I have had an e-mail from D [an officer at Thames Valley Police].

Ian

16.11.12

Ian

I am away for work at present but will continue to deal with matters as soon as I return.

Best

18.11.12

Thanks for keeping me posted. I really do appreciate it.

All of this is close to home.

The immediate concern I have is that the mother of one of my sons' classmates told me her son knows KCC. He is 11 years old like my sons. The boy's horse is kept in a field next to Crookham's former playing fields.

This was before I knew what you told me. All I was aware of was his time in prison 40 years ago. I told her I was aware that KCC had some history and that it was a relationship that, if I were her, I wouldn't encourage. I told her no more. There's nothing more I can safely tell her at this stage.

All the best to you.

Ian

18.11.12

Ian

I understand your concern. I was unaware that he had spent time in prison. I assume that was for offences committed on minors? If that is the case it seems so wrong that he is still allowed access to children.

Best

19.11.12

I don't know why he was in prison. In the cutting from the paper I sent you, it said it was for fraud. I just knew he had been inside.

His crime (whatever it was) was in the late '60s before the sex offenders' register anyway. At the moment, there are no restrictions on him. You have told me he sexually abused you. So he needs to be charged with these offences and the law will take its course. When he is found guilty, there will be a custodial sentence and he will be on the sex offenders' register, so we will all know he is not allowed near children.

At this moment, he is totally free. But he's a sexual abuser who should be nowhere near children. You have trusted me with this information. There's nothing I can do with it. You need to make a complaint to the police—and, yes, this requires courage. You left it for 37 years and I know why abused children don't disclose. You have disclosed to me. You need to do it to the police.

If you want to talk it through, here I am.

Best.

Ian

19.11.12

That newspaper article re KCC stated he was 51? Surely that cannot be correct? After all I was 50 yesterday

Best

19.11.12

Congratulations on reaching your half-century!

The article was from some years ago when he was, indeed, 51. I think he's 68 now. Age is no barrier, in my experience. Cadman was in his mid-70s when he was imprisoned.

I know that he is a regular visitor to the psychiatric hospital over the road. I am pretty sure that he has tutees. I would find it really difficult to have a conversation with him to elicit this now, knowing what I now know.

What you have told me he has done makes him dangerous. Please tell the Cheshire police what happened to you. There really is no need to feel bad about delaying this for so long. No one will blame you for it. No one blamed Andy—and his disclosure was before the current Savile enquiry. Abused children will cope with their abuse in various ways. Remaining silent for decades is one of them.

Best.

Ian

05.12.12

G'day.

Any news?

Ian

05.12.12

Ian

Currently waiting for some advice from a very old friend who is a lawyer in London

Best

06.12.12

Thank you for keeping in touch. I do appreciate it. Because I know something that no one else here knows, with every day that goes by I am starting to feel the silence.

There has been an important legal development at this end.

Historic abuse is very much on the radar these days with some TV presenters being arrested for offences dating back in some cases 50 years. Today, it's announced that judges are being advised to take into account when sentencing both the nature of the crime itself and the psychological effects on the victim resulting from the crime.

If your friend is an expert on historic abuse, that's great. If not, I can give you the number of a lawyer who is. As I'm sure they will tell you, the only morally correct way ahead is for police to be informed and for the victim to let the law take its course with the perpetrator. Otherwise an abuser is left free to do as he wishes.

Best.

Ian

06.12.12

Ian

I understand your concern. It is going to happen not because of what happened in the past to me but the fact it may be still happening and that deeply concerns me.

06.01.13

Any news on your timescale?

I haven't been to Crookham since you told me about Coulson. My boys are starting to ask about "Keith".

It's hard to keep silent …

Ian

06.13.13

Ian

Currently away on summer vacation. Will be back in Sydney after 18th jan. Moving house the week after. I understand your urgency so I plan to act soonest

Regards

06.01.13

Thanks. I appreciate your keeping in contact.

Let me know if there's anything I can do to help.

Best.

Ian

21.01.13

Ian

I have received the legal advice required to proceed. I shall contact the Cheshire police within the next few days. It has been a very busy time of late and we are moving house this week so we have 17 years of junk to move. Plus it is our summer holiday currently. I will keep you posted of progress and will mention your involvement in assisting me in this.

Regards

10.02.13

Has it happened?

Ian

11.02.13

Hopefully this week

13.02.13

It's OK. D. mailed me yesterday. Cheshire have been in contact with her.

Best.

Ian

21.02.13

Ian,

I am in the process of looking for a point of contact with NSW police in order that a statement can be taken here for Cheshire police. I have not heard back from the officer handling the case apart from her initial e-mail. Obviously these things take time and are clearly not a huge priority. Hopefully police involvement will prevent KCC having access to any children as this is my deepest concern not really the events of the past. I am not a believer in coincidence and the fact that he has been involved with Crookham Court in the past really does sound alarm bells.

As yet I have not informed my family. This is a dilemma as my mother is not well and we do have one sister still in the uk organising nursing homes etc. I do not want to burden them with these issues especially given that my mother may feel (although totally unwarranted) some guilt as I was sent to Terra Nova when my father took up a job in Brunei.

Thank you for your ongoing support it is much appreciated.

Best

21.02.13

Thank you for keeping me updated. I have no idea about anything as I have not been to Crookham Court since you told me what happened, although an old boy who is making a film about the School has Cavendish-Coulson on camera telling how the owners of the School told him to destroy all the records. I have communicated this to D. along with the name of a boy who spent much time with him.

I think it's an excellent idea that you make contact with your local police as an "official" link with the UK and make a statement.

I have asked D. if she can make any other suggestion.

The wheels of justice grind slowly. Nevertheless, what you have revealed is serious and really does need to be actioned. D. was heartened that Cheshire police contacted her so quickly. It may well be that things are happening behind the scenes. I do hope so. I'll let you know when I hear from her.

I understand your concern. My experience is that the predominant parental feeling is not one of guilt. The disclosure is seen as the child trusting the parent. After all, the parent wasn't to know and while there may be sorrow that it went unspoken at the time, it is accepted as the normal reaction of a child. You are opening up the secret guilt and the more this happens, the less secret the crime becomes and the more it will become the norm for children to disclose at the time.

We keep in touch.

Best.

Ian

21.02.13

D. has replied to me and is taking action.

Best.

Ian

21.02.13

Here is a message I have just received from Cheshire police.

Would you like to respond to J?

Best.

Ian

Rob was a man I had never met, never spoken to, and who lived 12,000 miles away. Over the months of email correspondence, we had struck up a relationship and he felt able to confide in me. That our correspondence was all on record made it easy for the police as there was no question of who said what to whom. In September 2013, KCC was duly charged with "19 counts of indecent assault against boys under 14, which relate to four victims between 1973 and 1975." Cheshire police issued a press release:

> "The investigation is continuing and is focussed upon Cavendish-Coulson's employment both as a public school teacher, and a private tutor at establishments across the country over the course of his working life."

The following month:

> "70 year old Keith Cavendish-Coulson of Berkshire was re-arrested on 10 October 2013, and subsequently charged

> with a further 16 counts of indecent assault against three young boys. He will appear at Crewe Magistrates on 29 October 2013.
>
> "Cavendish-Coulson was previously charged with 19 counts of indecent assault against boys under 14, which relate to four victims between 1973 and 1975 back in August this year. It brings the total number of charges to 35, relating to seven victims."

By the end of 2013, the number of counts had increased to 57. In 2014 it had reached 97. All this from a few mentions on a Facebook page and a search on Google.

And by that time, I had met Rob Harding. His mother had died and he came over for her funeral. He visited Cheshire police and, on the way back, came to see me. I was in the throes of my summer school and was surrounded by children. He saw them play the "Slave Auction". The incongruity was not lost on him. Here were children thoroughly enjoying their childhood. We spoke in the boardroom of the Mary Hare School with one of my sons popping in from time to time wondering why Daddy wasn't joining in the fun. He spoke to me in general terms about the abuse and how he was dealing with it and, although it was as different from the other cases as each case is different from every other one, the effect it had on the victim was exactly the same. The tone of voice, the expression, the body language were identical to those I had heard before. This fifty-year-old man I was meeting for the first time was telling me that the very core of his being had been touched when he was a small boy and the feeling had never left him.

He did not go into the details of the crimes perpetrated against him, although I later read what abuse all his victims had suffered in the opening note of the sentencing hearing at Chester Crown Court in November 2014.

It would not be long, however, before I was to be made aware personally of this man's modus operandi.

SEVENTEEN

Abuse comes close to home

I sensed that Cavendish-Coulson had not begun abusing at Terra Nova in 1973 and that, had he started earlier, he would have been abusing at Crookham Court. In September 2014 two events occurred that brought into sharp relief either the difference in attitudes that forty years can bring, or how circumstances can be handled so differently that the outcomes are poles apart. At 07.35 one morning, my thirteen-year-old son Lars's text to me read, "We r off to school now." It was his new school. A huge public school and very different from his prep school. At 10.35, he texted, "I am doing well." An hour later, the medical centre called me to say he had been brought to them with a headache and blurred vision. An hour after that, he texted, "Please take me out of here forever." "Why?" I replied. "I hate every aspect of this place. I have no friends. There is too much work. There are too many children. I get bullied and the teachers don't listen to me." A succession of texts followed. "I am at the lowest point of my life right now. I would rather die than be at this establishment 5 more years." Then, "I can't wait to get home and escape the worst place I've ever been to. Please help me. I can't stop crying."

When Lars came home, he told me what had happened after his 10.35 text. "We went into a house meeting. There were more than 100 people there. The sixth-formers were at the back wearing their suits. I came in with M." M was a boy he had met at nursery and had been friends with until they went to different primary schools. Time, distance, and life had got in the way since then and it was only when they had met at an induction day the term before that they realised they would be in the same form and the same house. "He recognised me at once," Lars had said. "I'll know someone there." They walked into the meeting together. "There's Ginger with his boyfriend," came a voice from the mass of grey-suited sixth-formers.

When he returned home that evening, Lars sobbed, "If they're like that at the top of the school, what are the rest like?" My fingers twitched and quickly went to the keyboard. I told his housemaster what had happened, quoted his texts to me, and ended:

> "This is why Lars' next text mentioned bullying. He has never before encountered this sort of gratuitous animosity or casual homophobia. I have always told my sons that it's no one's business but theirs whom they choose to fall in love with—not that this has any connection with what was said or why the words were spoken."

I received a prompt reply (email, 2 September 2014):

> "I am very sorry to hear about this and can quite understand that Lars would be upset by this, particularly on his first morning at the school. This is most certainly not the kind of behaviour that we condone and I shall be speaking to all of my sixth formers most strongly in the morning. If the boy who did this can be identified then I can assure you that appropriate action will be taken."

The next day Lars's tutor took him for a short walk which happened to pass a house where there was a lady standing by an open door making a cup of tea. They were invited in. Lars's tutor left.

"She's very nice," said Lars. "She told me I could come and talk to her when I wanted."

She was the school counsellor and he saw her a couple of times before he asked me to come, too. She gave him coping mechanisms—"You have the power to change situations"—and over the weeks found that one of the reasons for not relinquishing his sad feelings was his attachment to me and the feeling that, if he let go, something bad might happen to me. "You aren't going to make him live any longer. In fact, if he has to worry about you, the opposite may be true."

The corner was being turned and a sad thirteen year old was becoming his old self again.

At exactly this time, I received a friend request on Facebook from a boy I used to teach. I recognised the name immediately and accepted his request with the message, "Hello again—after a decade or three ... Good to hear from you." In fact, it was nearer four decades. His response was almost immediate. I was on a train. My calls were diverted to my mobile phone. It rang and a voice told me that this was the boy who had made contact. It was an old voice, a guarded voice without the warmth that a natural intonation conveys. It spoke of constraint, of being unused to communicating on a personal level and, while it became somewhat more relaxed as the conversation proceeded, it remained a whine. I instantly recalled the face of the thirteen year old whose voice it was.

(Telephone conversation, 9 September 2014): "I googled Crookham Court last night." He paused, unsure how to introduce what was going to be a significant conversation. "A lot's been going on. I found your page and read about what's been happening."

"Yes, quite a bit."

"The thing is that what's been done was done to me. It ruined my life."

It was a complaining voice. It contained regret and more than a little resentment. Here we go again, a life in pieces. He had a right to complain.

Before Robert had a chance to say another word, I interrupted. "Tell the police."

"Oh yes, I've done that. I also called Charles Derham. That's how I got your number."

There was no need for cajoling; no circumlocution. This boy—for that is how I saw him, frozen in time at thirteen—had seen the film in which Andy, looking straight at the camera, described factually and unemotionally every detail of what had been done to which parts of his body. That Keith Cavendish-Coulson was facing ninety-seven counts of sexual assault on boys is what had given him his courage. He was not a lone voice. He also knew that he could be direct with me.

"Shall I call you 'Mr. Mucklejohn'?"

"No, you're a grown-up now."

"Yes. I'm fifty-six. Look, do you remember the baths downstairs? In that long room right under the staff room? That's where it started. There was a line of them. No doors, walls, or curtains, or anything. No privacy, we just had our—what was it?—weekly?—yes, I think weekly bath there and he used to come in. 'Anyone want his back scrubbed?' he'd say and then he just washed my back anyway. He asked me to come up and have coffee in his room and I went up. That's where it happened. Somehow he got his hands on my underwear, said 'That's nice', then he got into my underwear and onto my cock. He masturbated me. Made me masturbate him. He shoved his penis in my mouth, came all over me. I can still smell his cum. Later on, he tried to get his penis up my arse, but he couldn't manage it, so he shoved his finger up my arse and then made me do the same with him and I had to suck my finger."

The line went dead. We had entered a tunnel. I called back.

"Sorry, Robert, I'm on a train and the signal may go, but keep on. What you're telling me is serious stuff. How often did this happen?"

"Oh, practically every day. Sometimes twice a day—in the afternoon and evening. Sometimes, at lunch. You know I was at the table just down from the staff table? [Name redacted] would sit next to me and say, "I've got something for you in my pocket," and I'd have to sit there very close to him with my hand in his pocket and masturbate him. He'd just sit there in the middle of the dining room while I jerked him off. No one noticed."

"I had no idea, Robert."

"You were on the staff table and it was happening a few yards away from where you were. It wasn't only in term-time either. You know I wasn't any good at school work." I remembered this. I was seeing a very slim boy, willowy and ethereal as though anything stronger than a light breeze would blow him over. He was as white as a corpse and had a skin condition. He spent some days in sick bay with a mystery illness. Everything was slotting into place. "Well, my parents said I needed a tutor in the Easter holidays and they employed this man."

"You didn't say 'no'?"

"Couldn't. My father would've known something was up and would've beaten me. He was an alcoholic by then. If the dog shat on the carpet, it'd be my fault and he'd rub my face in it. He was just nasty. [Name redacted] would take me into his room, the guest room we had, and he'd abuse me there in my parents' house."

"And no one knew? No one saw anything?"

"My father came in once and he made out he was doing something else. I think he thought it was odd, but he didn't bother."

"Were there any other boys involved?"

By this time, Robert was as forthcoming as he could be. I was simply eliciting information. It was yet another variation on a tragic theme. He needed to externalise his trauma. Only it was forty years too late. There was a twist that I had not expected, though. "He abused another boy at the same time as me. He was a small boy. Blond. I think he was a first former. Can't remember his name, but he's in the photo, second from the right, front row. He had me come upstairs with him and made us do it to him together and then he made me masturbate the boy and made the boy suck me off. And then that man went down on me. Poor kid. He was terrified. Think he left soon after this. When it was all over we just cuddled together. We hugged each other. For support; for comfort. We weren't doing anything else. I'm not gay."

"Did you say anything to each other?"

"Not really. We both thought it was the way of the world. It was just the way things were."

A thirteen year old and an eleven year old thought that gross abuse and rape were just the way things were. At Crookham Court School in 1973, they were completely right.

"I think of this all the time, you know."

"I can imagine you do. You know that you're the victim of many serious assaults. You need to relate all this to the police. I'll try and find out who the boy is. He's a material witness. You know you need counselling."

"Look, Ian, I haven't got two pennies to rub together."

I checked on the compensation situation. Crookham Court's renamed holding company, Cape Argus, had become insolvent. There was the school building awaiting redevelopment, or demolition if the local yobs managed to burn it down, in a deal that must have been worth millions and there was not a penny for the victims. That was the way things were.

"I've thought of suicide. Most days. Tried it. I'm on lots of pills. I just took them all. It's true. It ruins your life. Now I'll ruin his."

This slight young man I had last seen at the age of sixteen was achieving a passion that had been decades in the making.

"Did you tell him to stop? Tell him you'd report him?"

"Yes, I told him to stop. It just went on and on. It was horrible, all these things he made me do. I told him I'd tell someone about him. He told me no one would believe me and that he'd tell the headmaster that I had made a move on him, that I'd tried it on with him. He's a real bastard. I visited Crookham about seven years ago. I met a man who said he knew him. Said he was a sweet old man." The contempt, the hatred was coming out. "I've got no confidence. Lost all that at Crookham Court. I've never felt right since I left that place."

"Look, Robert, you have to know that it was never your fault. You were the victim then. You are the victim now. You can see justice done. You must never blame yourself. None of this was caused by you. You have had terrible things done to you and how your body reacted was purely physiological."

I told Robert that I would be there for him, if he wished, and that I would try to track down the other boy. Using the scraps of information I had retained from my days there, I recollected his name and, again using Facebook, I found him. Should I contact him there and then to tell him he could contact me if there was anything he wished to say? I decided against and gave the information to Robert, assuming the police would follow up information about this material witness and fellow victim.

After this, Robert disappeared from Facebook and his phone remained on permanent answering machine. Perhaps in his anxiety to unburden, he felt he had told me too much. Maybe the police had warned him not to say any more. I had to assume that it was his choice to sever his connection and I respected it. When he was being forthcoming, I asked him if I might include him in this book. "What I hope for, Robert, is that everyone will know that these crimes happen and that the thing to do is tell someone in the knowledge that action will result." He readily agreed to be included.

Yet again, abuse had defined a life. The modus operandi was different in this case as it was with all of them, but the anger, the bitterness, the touching of the deepest recesses of the soul were all identical. I knew there had to have been a Crookham connection. Here it was. I had not imagined it would have been Robert, but he had all the qualifications—a shy, gauche, lonely boy, not one with friends who would wonder where he was. A child who was unnoticed, anonymous. A suggestible boy who would simply do as he was told. Robert had no idea about sex before he was stripped of his innocence. At his hands, he had his first sexual experiences and every one was a perversion and brutalisation of the act of lovemaking. "Don't think badly of me," he pleaded.

And there was my shy, gauche, lonely Lars at his new school. Had such a teacher taken an interest in him I had a good idea what could have happened.

On 16 May 2015 I emailed the chief constable of Cheshire:

> My connection with this case is that I obtained the original disclosure from Rob Harding which led to the investigation and conviction of Keith Cavendish-Coulson on 25 counts of abuse at Terra Nova School and elsewhere.
>
> On 09.09.2014, [name redacted], who was a pupil at Crookham Court School when [name redacted] was teaching there prior to his appointment at [name redacted], disclosed to me two years of abuse by [name redacted] at Crookham Court School, Thatcham, Berkshire and at his home when he was tutored by [name redacted] in the holidays. He also disclosed that the abuse involved another boy whose name he did not remember but whose position on a school photograph from that period he pinpointed, enabling me to identify the other child involved. [Name redacted] told me he was due to give a statement to Cheshire Police on 11.09.2014.

> I have not heard anything since.
>
> I wonder if you could tell me if the case is proceeding and if you would like the identity of the victim [name redacted] disclosed to me.

In October 2015, I re-sent the e-mail and was telephoned to be told that statements had been taken. I gave the name of the boy who had frequented his room.

While I was speaking, I remembered—and related to the police—that the boy's mum had met me after he had left the school. "You know," she had reflected, "My son was never the same after Crookham Court."

EIGHTEEN

The Cavendish-Coulson trial

Keith Cavendish-Coulson received six years and nine months in prison on forty-five specimen counts against twenty-five boys, twenty-four of whom were boarders at Terra Nova School. At his sentencing, the school was described as a harsh environment with rigid, military-style discipline and bullying. Coulson was the soft-spoken, gentle teacher, colourfully dressed who, if you were one of his favourites, would invite you into his room. This touch of domesticity was a far cry from the bleak environment of the school. Soft furnishings, a carpet under your feet, warmth from a fire, tea, biscuits, all the comforts of home. Boy after boy wrote about how they wanted this attention. In the classroom, he was attentive, too, offering extra help by his desk.

An occasion in the dispassionate language of the court opening notes at his sentencing (all extracts from a court document dated 13 October 2014) is typical of what happened to one eight year old in a lesson: "Y [Coulson] stood BR between his legs whilst sitting sideways on to BR, unzipped BR's trousers and masturbated BR who did not ejaculate. After this he took BR's hand and placed it onto his own penis outside of his trousers. This happened three or four times and each time it followed the same pattern. BR stated that during these episodes he felt terrified and scared. He knew that it was wrong but did not know what to do. He did not tell anyone at school about it."

In the classroom, in the dormitory, and in Coulson's private room, boy after boy from the age of eight to thirteen had this done to him and then he had to place his hands on Coulson's erect penis. He was their teacher. He showed them kindness and he made them to do this. They had no idea about sex until Coulson abused them. This confusion at an early age left victims with long-term psychological damage with several describing the impact the man's behaviour had on them. One victim wrote:

> The school was a violent, authoritarian place. Bullying was rife and corporal punishment was common. It was a dreadful place. It was the 1970s, but more like *Tom Brown's School Days*.
>
> It was in this kind of environment that Keith Cavendish-Coulson befriended me. He was kind to me.
>
> He spoke to me softly and gently. He took advantage of my neediness, my vulnerability and instead of looking after me he used me for his own sexual gratification and he groomed me.
>
> I knew it was wrong and horrible what he was doing, but I was completely unable to stop him. I felt totally frozen and horrified. It was humiliating. Sometimes it was also physically painful ... but I didn't feel capable of telling anyone.
>
> I can say with absolute certainty that the experience of being sexually abused by Keith Cavendish-Coulson had a devastating effect on my life. Most of the time I am an emotional wreck, lacking self-esteem, plagued by depression.

Familiar sentiments, eloquently expressed and heartfelt.

In a ghastly story, what stands out as being utterly horrifying is that this could have been stopped dead because the school knew what was happening. The then headmaster had permitted Coulson to continue after a boy had reported inappropriate touching and his successor promised action to a concerned parent, but did not act until some time later, writing:

> "I know that he may have done a great deal of damage to boys—he has also done a great deal of damage to himself … . It would do untold damage to the school if parents wished to take proceedings against Mr. Coulson and I think the quicker we can forgive and forget the better …"

A doctor to whom Coulson was sent after complaints wrote: "I have discussed this matter fully with my colleagues at the practice and we all feel that the matter should be dropped. I think it would be extremely difficult to circularise the parents of such an exclusive school and stir up a lot of trouble unnecessarily. I hope you agree with this view."

This indeed was the view of many professional bodies at the time—to keep secrets and preserve their reputation.

The school was far more interested in preserving its reputation than letting the truth be told. The records show that the headmaster's successor heard from several schools that Coulson was either applying for a job (Slindon College) or wanted to tutor privately (Eton) or was actually teaching (St. John's Beaumont) on at least one occasion with a faked reference. On 21 November 1977 Coulson's name was placed at the time on what was known as "List 99", a list of people barred from working with children in state education. In 1994, the list was amended to include prohibitions on people working in the private education sector. In July 2010, he was transferred to the modern equivalent "The Children's Barred List" which prevents individuals from working with children within regulated activity, including education. A breach of a prohibition constitutes a criminal offence. Nevertheless, the report makes clear that Coulson "remained determined to work in education". And this is just what he did for decades. Had there been a prosecution in the mid-'70s, this would likely have put a stop to him.

Justice had to wait forty years to be done. Again, it was the courage of a victim—a child's voice from the past—that brought the truth into the open. Paedophiles do not suddenly stop being paedophiles. That there were more victims during that time is a near certainty.

Lonely children away from home who responded to kindness and warmth. A school that let an offender move on. It was Crookham Court in the north. No wonder Coulson was attracted to it in the first place and knew afterwards that he could simply move from school to school until he found one that didn't bother to check.

After the verdict, Rob wrote on the "Survivors" Facebook page. He used his real name, even though his family still had no idea about events in the UK. (Facebook, 24 December 2014):

> Social media is often much maligned, especially by those of my vintage. However, if it had not been for the Survivors of Crookham Court Facebook page, a serial paedophile would have escaped justice for a lifetime of abuse on the young boys in his charge.
>
> I have spent a lifetime forcing the memories of events at Terra Nova school to the deepest, furthest recesses of my mind in a futile attempt to rid myself of the shame, guilt, self loathing and anger that I have endured as a result of the abuse I was subject to at that school. For a number of reasons those memories in recent years ceased to be dormant and began to haunt me: firstly because I made a decision to visit the school some 5 years ago which was deeply traumatic and triggered a multitude of bad memories. Secondly my son is now 9: I look at him and imagine how I may feel should I unknowingly grant the care of my child to an abuser. I imagine the guilt would be unbearable. Thirdly, my father died some 6 years ago and

my mother passed away in 2013. Thus I no longer feel the need to protect them from the inevitable guilt they would have felt should I have disclosed the fact that, whilst they were living 10,000 miles away on the other side of the world, the school they had entrusted to educate and care for me was actively covering up the fact that one of their teachers had been sexually abusing many of the boys.

So I went searching on the internet for a Keith Cavendish Coulson. This search quickly brought me to the Survivors of Crookham Court Facebook page. I read with horror that Coulson had some involvement with a school so infamous for its abuse of young boys that even someone who has spent the last 27 years living on the other side of the world was aware of it. I found his address, which was duly noted in preparation for my next visit to the UK. Luckily I then came into contact with Ian Mucklejohn via the Survivors page. We exchanged e-mails over a number of months and I decided to firstly disclose the abuse I had been subjected to by Coulson to Ian and then report this abuse to the Cheshire Police.

Without the selfless support and help from Ian I very much doubt this whole case would have eventuated in finally bringing Coulson to justice. It has been a hard road: none of my family is aware of the case. I have never disclosed this abuse to anyone. However, once faced with the possibility Coulson might still be abusing, the decision to make a statement to the police became elementary. At that time I was utterly unaware that there had been previous abuse charges against Coulson that had failed.

So much of my behavior in early adulthood I now understand comes from the abuse I received at the hands of Coulson. Much of my attitude to authority stems from the way Terra Nova dealt with the knowledge of this abuse. It is not an uncommon reaction and the harsh reality is that nearly all institutional responses to sexual abuse be they schools or churches have been denial and cover up.

It has taken a lifetime to realize how utterly traumatic it was being sent to Terra Nova: I was homesick; my parents were on the other side of the world; I was bullied both by other boys and by the Headmaster's wife, Mrs. Best. Her treatment of those she disliked was vindictive, capricious and fundamentally evil. She took pleasure in humiliating young boys for no other reason than she possibly had an inkling you were not totally and utterly compliant. What a perfect storm of misery it was for a new teacher to enter the fray, who offered friendliness where there was only punishment, misery and humiliation at the hands of those in charge. What a perfect time and place to groom your victims. It does not surprise me that the school attempted to brush the multiple episodes of abuse under the carpet. After all the school had its reputation to maintain and that was clearly more important than the well-being of the boys entrusted to their care. It doesn't surprise me because I am a cynic. I expect the worst of people. I have never had trust or faith in anyone in a position of authority since I was 11 years old.

The process of giving evidence and dealing with the Police investigation from the other side of the world has been clearly stressful, but the support I received from Ian Mucklejohn throughout this period has been invaluable. Given my cynical propensity to authority, I have nothing but absolute praise for the Cheshire Police and the team of detectives I have dealt with. The investigation teams have been assiduous, caring, compassionate and understanding throughout.

I must have exchanged dozens of e-mails with Ian Mucklejohn over the last 2 years. His being there to offer advice, assistance and moral support has been invaluable. It has made all the difference and I am deeply grateful to him.

> Coulson had 26 victims from Terra Nova and was charged with over 90 offences. Given the modus operandi of abusers, there are undoubtedly other victims out there. He spent a lifetime abusing. Disclosure is not easy, but from my own perspective I not only believe I did the right thing, but have destroyed some of those demons that have haunted me for 40 years. I wish I had been able to come forward at the time of the abuse or soon after as it may have prevented further abuse but, given the finer details of the case exposed post trial, a great deal of the guilt I have carried has been lifted. I have been in contact with old school friends from Terra Nova and it has been cathartic to at last be able to talk with those who also suffered at that school.
>
> Survivors of Crookham Court has been pivotal in finally ensuring Coulson now resides in a place he cannot abuse children. To all those involved in maintaining and contributing to the page—well done.

One of the replies, this one from Andy, read (Facebook, 24 December 2014):

> Sitting here in Costa Coffee in town with tears welling up after reading this. Having been through a similar process a few years ago I know how it feels. The elation of finally telling someone after years of hiding it is truly life changing.
>
> I also agree without Ian Mucklejohn I don't think I would have the courage to see it through. My advice. Is get some therapy and it must be a long term project too or you will hit a wall like my self.
>
> Well done for standing up.

Rob and Andy had no hesitation in giving me permission to use their real names in this book. While not all their demons have been exorcised yet, both of them found disclosure a liberating experience.

NINETEEN

Two new boys

A Crookham Court music teacher was on Henry Scott's (not his real name) mind when he came to see me in May 2013. As soon as I received the friend request on Facebook, I sensed what lay behind it and responded at once with "Yes, I remember you. You were there with Adam Wilson [not his real name]." It was in association with this teacher that I remembered him. In those days it was unremarkable that he should have been so often in the company of this brown-haired, softly-spoken bearded man in his mid-20s engaging, as I assumed, in their shared passion for church music and discussions on religiosity during their evenings in his small bedsit in the school, Adam Wilson's scouse twang gently expounding his views to his admiring audience of one. Henry was a rather intense child, blond, well-built, and serious for his fifteen years; his mouth a straight line and his eyes like boreholes.

Henry responded immediately with a phone number and was sitting on my sofa the following day. Adam Wilson's brown hair extended to the rest of his body, Henry told me. It was a body he had come to know well.

"We're both new boys," Wilson had brightly told Henry on the day they both arrived, new to Crookham Court, on that sunny September afternoon. "We shall have to look out for each other." Henry had told him of his interest in music and the church and was immediately invited to his room for earnest discussions. Within a few days, the thirteen year old was on his sofa with his trousers and pants down and his penis in the man's mouth. Henry apologised to him. It was the first time he had an orgasm and he thought he had wet himself. He didn't know what was happening but, as he put it to me, he liked the feeling.

"You were taken in. You were a child. He was using you. Your body was reacting to the stimuli it was receiving."

He told me he didn't have to go up those stairs.

The feelings were the same as had been described by others. Here was the guilt that had wracked him for decades. He had brought it all on himself. This thirteen year old had chosen to go up the stairs in the full knowledge of what would happen. He had his own key. For two years, Henry was the object of Adam Wilson's attentions.

Henry described to me how he had taken him on visits, to concerts, and given him presents. It fed into Wilson's delusions of grandeur that he was at a public school. He came to know the boy's grandparents, visited them at their home, became almost a family member.

And all this time "full-on buggery" was taking place.

Henry told me about another teacher and how this one had come into Wilson's room and talked in front of him about the physical attributes of boys he fancied.

"So this other teacher knew what was happening? Knew you were being abused?"

"Oh yes."

Adam Wilson would take him on visits to churches around the country where he would be asked to sing in the choirs. They went to stay at his parents' house while they were away. He bathed him in their bath and whilst in there he masturbated him. They visited a church nearby and he sang in the choir. They stayed with one of Wilson's male friends in his three bedroom semi-detached house. If ever they stayed overnight, Wilson and he would share a bed. When they were in Cambridge they stayed in a student's room. The student was called Ralph O'Mahoney (not his real name).

They visited country house hotels and drank alcohol and travelled to Soho in London to buy books. They would meet Wilson's male friends and it felt as if he was being shown off or paraded in front of them. In one of the books Adam Wilson gave him to read, he remembered a story about a teacher loving a student and then eventually committing suicide.

He spoke of how the horror of the abuse made him bury things in such a deep place that he did not think about them, and how the deep emotional conditioning and the place one finds oneself in carry on into everyday adult life and you find it impossible to confront any kind of problem or unpleasantness, so you bury it deep down with all the other stuff. How on the surface you develop a gregarious persona as a façade. You don't want anyone knowing; it's too embarrassing, too painful. If you dwell on them, the images become too graphic and of course it's all your fault, not his. You did those things. You were there. And how it becomes your way of coping with everything in life. You have no close friendships; no one is allowed near.

This man started his first adult sexual relationship at the age of forty-five.

A few years ago, Adam Wilson was found dead at his home. The verdict was suicide. He had been on police bail following his arrest after allegations of sexual abuse at another school.

Henry told me about how, that January, he had contemplated suicide. How he walked into a doctor's surgery and asked to see a doctor "at once". The doctor was kind and called him from time to time. He had been told not to embark on counselling before the trial.

"I think that's changed, or changing."

He had been reckless when he was young. He didn't care whether he lived or died.

Henry was an articulate man who wanted to know how he had reached where he was at the age of forty-nine; whether he would be in this place had he not been seduced at the start of puberty. He had entered the priesthood in which he assumed there was no sex at all so that he could sort himself out. Even there, he had not been safe. He was "anointed" in a "special room", he told me. He had to be naked as a sign that he had renounced worldly goods. The oil was placed low down in his pubic area. Eventually, he told the police. The bishop was subsequently arrested.

His religious concepts of sin and guilt added to the self-loathing he felt. He wanted to go back to who he had been; to those places that nature's safety valve closes us off from; to discover who he was and who he would have been. He needed to get to the truth through the blur of alcohol and denial that had been his life—his loveless life as a boy and a man.

He knew it would be awful, but the not knowing was even worse.

"It's dangerous, Henry. I think we forget for a reason."

At forty-nine, Henry was unemployed, isolated from his family, and incontinent. "I closed my business," he told me in January 2014. He had had no income since then. He had discussed none of this with his wife and she continued to think that he was away at the office when, in fact, he was sitting in his car the whole day.

He wondered what he would be doing if he hadn't gone to that school.

For Henry, the actions of that music teacher at that school more than thirty-five years before had defined his life. His parents were abroad and had not noticed. His grandparents had been so flattered by the attentions of such a cultivated and learned young man who seemed to be giving their grandson remarkable opportunities that they must have assumed any change in behaviour was because of these vistas of civilisation that were opening up. It took years for Henry to see that he was simply being used for sex, that all the relationships he could have developed never happened and that, at the age of forty-nine, his former English teacher who had not seen him since the age of fifteen was the person in his life he had known the longest and to whom he confided these intimate details. His parents remain unaware to this day. Eventually, without a word from the teacher, the pupil would simply get naked and be buggered. There was no force. He had simply been manoeuvred.

More than counselling, to know exactly what had happened was what he wanted. Only then, he felt, when he had remembered who he had been and what had been done to him, could the healing process begin and only when he was able to revisit his past could he help bring to justice those who had taken his childhood from him.

And I knew that I had seen it while it was happening. Had seen the two of them on Wilson's bed, chatting, books spread over the cover, classical music in the background. A man of twenty-five and a boy of thirteen who looked perfectly at ease with other. And nothing had struck me as strange.

TWENTY

Shandy at the pub

Ralph O'Mahoney (not his real name) was a boy of nineteen when he came to Crookham Court School in January 1978. He was a sportsman and a history scholar on his way from school to Cambridge. He wanted to do a gap year and responded to an advertisement Cadman placed for such a vacancy. Tall, gangly, young-looking and so only just-out-of-school that he didn't know how to write a cheque, he was an unlikely child-abuser and it was more than a decade before I realised this is what he was. He stayed at Crookham Court only until July 1978, loving every moment, he told me, when he went up to Cambridge to study history. On graduating, he became a history teacher at a noted HMC school. The HMC is the Headmasters' and Headmistresses' Conference, an organisation that the heads of most prestigious independent schools belong to—private schools but usually and perhaps oddly termed public schools, as most of the public would be prohibited from attending by the fees which generally exceed the average annual salary. Private education enjoys a great deal of freedom from the constraints imposed on the state sector. This includes the freedom to appoint whoever they wish to teaching posts. O'Mahoney then applied for and was appointed head of history at an HMC school in Wales from

January 1988. That April, I received a letter from him, not from Wales, but from New Zealand. He told me he had decided on a change. I asked him what had happened and eventually discovered that he had been dismissed just before he would have left and that, in his words, he had "run away to the wilds of New Zealand". He told me he had hit a boy. The headmaster had told the school which had appointed him of his dismissal and the offered job had been withdrawn, leaving Ralph facing unemployment. So, Ralph contra mundum obtained a teaching job at a small school in Wanganui, then at a prestigious school in Auckland. As an HMC member, that school could appoint whoever it wished and it wished to appoint Ralph O'Mahoney.

Two years later, I was sending out invitations to a reception I was holding in a local hotel at which Esther Rantzen would talk to parents and past pupils about the *That's Life!* investigations into Crookham Court School that resulted in the arrest and conviction of Cadman and two other teachers and the closure of the school. I received a telephone call from one of the old boys, Jed Nilssen (not his real name), who called partly to accept and partly to drop a small bombshell. "I just want your assurance about something," he said. "Tell me that one of the teachers who taught me when I was a boy at Crookham isn't in teaching any longer." Quite a few names raced through my mind, but the one he came up with took me by surprise. "Ralph O'Mahoney," he told me.

Jed remembered Ralph O'Mahoney well. He went on to tell me that one summer's day in 1978, he was taken out in Ralph O'Mahoney's car. Both of us recalled the car clearly for its incongruity. It was a lavender Hillman Imp. They stopped at a pub. He bought Jed a lemonade. "Ralph O'Mahoney said to me, 'You know what Mr. Howe does to you when you go to see him in his bedroom. Would you like to do these things with me?'" Even though Jed had been only thirteen, he knew exactly what the man meant. "I said 'No' and the conversation just died," he said.

"That's odd," I answered. "I've just been to New Zealand to see Ralph. He was in some trouble and I became concerned for his well-being. It seems that he hit a child while he was a teacher. He was due to leave that school to become head of history elsewhere. The school sacked him because it was his second offence and the one he was going to cancelled his contract. He ended up flying off to New Zealand and he has a housemastership there. I told him that if he hits children he shouldn't be teaching. I told him so in letters and in person and he assured me he was thinking about other work. Look, Jed, I'll call the headmaster to see if it really was 'hitting' a child that he was sacked for and get back to you."

The then headmaster was uncompromising and told me there was no connection between the offence for which he was sacked and the allegation made by the Crookham Court schoolboy. He also told me that the offence for which he was dismissed was not the first.

I contacted Jed with this information and told him my opinion was that as it happened so long ago we should not take it further. Fortunately events took an unexpected turn that caused me to reassess my decision.

In our letters and conversations in New Zealand, Ralph had told me he was, indeed, looking for work outside teaching which would be less stressful. He put his assault on a pupil down to pressure. In light of this, I let him put my name as a referee on his CV which he promised would be used for jobs not in teaching. A head teacher in New Zealand wrote to me in August 1992 to ask for my opinion on Ralph O'Mahoney who was applying for a deputy headship. I contacted the head to tell him that the applicant had been dismissed from a UK school and suggested he contact the school to discover the reason. I also contacted Ralph to express my disappointment that he had used my name to try to secure a job in teaching.

The following month, I received a letter from the Department of Education and Science (28 September 1992). It told me my name had been given to them by Ralph O'Mahoney who was asking them to reconsider "... the decision made on 27 June 1989 that Mr. O'Mahoney was unsuitable to teach in any school or educational establishment maintained or assisted from public funds. This decision followed a report that while teaching at the [name redacted] School Mr. O'Mahoney indecently assaulted a 10-year-old boy ..."

I wrote to Ralph asking him to explain. He replied, "Please ignore the letter from the DES. This is being dealt with in New Zealand and by one ex-colleague teaching in England. The DES mistook names on my CV with those who they were supposed to refer to re the report. I will write to them concerning this."

Banned teachers, including those who had not been convicted, were placed on List 99. My further enquiries with the DES could not confirm that he was on List 99, it was so secret, although I knew I was safe in assuming that he wouldn't have asked to be taken off it if he wasn't on it in the first place. I told the DES how I had been lied to by O'Mahoney, how I had advised him to give up teaching, and how a boy from O'Mahoney's past had come forward to say he had been propositioned.

I also wrote to the former headmaster who had, by then, retired. He phoned me to say that, although the reason O'Mahoney was dismissed was not the same as the propositioning Jed had alleged, there was a similarity he had not disclosed to me at the time. He also told me that the incident for which he had been dismissed was not the first time there had been a complaint. He added that Ralph O'Mahoney had recently written to him asking for a reference and assured him he had been taken off List 99. Having checked with the Department of Education and Science, he found O'Mahoney was off List 99 only for those children above a certain age. He ended by saying he would not give O'Mahoney a reference and that he found his attitude "slippery". There had not been a court case as the boy's parents had not wanted to traumatise their child.

I apologised to Jed and told him we would act on this. So, what to do?

First of all I had to protect the children in O'Mahoney's house in New Zealand. When he had written to me about the assault, he said that the headmaster of the New Zealand school had "asked me to keep it a secret", so there was no point in telling the school. I contacted the head of teacher registration, Peter Barlow, in New Zealand and told him (fax, 8 February 1993). He told me (fax, 8 February 1993) he had never heard of List 99. They had a similar list in New Zealand that was freely available so he wrote to the Department of Education and Science in the UK for confirmation. None was forthcoming. He wrote several times with no response.

I tried social services in Auckland (fax, 9 May 1993). They told me (fax, 11 May 1993) that they could act only when they had "specific information about abuse or neglect".

In the meantime, O'Mahoney was in the UK trying to get his ban from teaching by the DES lifted. He wrote to me at the beginning of 1993 (letter, 11 January 1993) to say that his "interview at the DES went very well. I had four very positive references from people …" He also wrote, "I was advised (by the HM) to keep the precise details of the incident as secret as possible. I apologise for not informing you of all the details. However, my case has been complicated by the letter you wrote which the official from the DES had to discuss with me. Some of the references to Crookham Court (a different school in 1978) and your views on my suitability as a teacher were not helpful and out of date. I hope they do not cloud the issue as people change and I have certainly changed. I was certainly caught off guard by this."

I replied (letter, 13 January 1993) that I didn't know what he had changed from.

In one of his faxes to me, Peter Barlow (9 February 1993) opined that "public knowledge of such a situation could be very damaging". Of course. The public only know about something if they are told. Television. I wrote to TVNZ in the UK (letter, 5 December 1993). I later found out from them that in 1993, TVNZ in the UK was "one man and a dog, except there's no dog". For months I heard nothing; 1993 slipped into 1994.

"Come now. This afternoon." Bryher Scudamore at the BBC's *That's Life!* meant business. Within hours of my telling her the story, TVNZ were on the phone from Auckland. Within weeks their investigations had started. Within months, in May 1994, they were in my garden filming me.

Ralph O'Mahoney was aware that TVNZ were making enquiries and left NZ with his head's permission to go on "study leave" in the UK. The presenter from TVNZ's *60 Minutes* was on his trail and, having interviewed and filmed Jed and me, was very keen to get him on camera. Earlier in May, O'Mahoney had visited me to find out what TVNZ was doing with the story. On that sunny afternoon, he had sat on my sofa and told me how ghastly it all was, the uncertainty, and how, if I did not do what I could to "depersonalise" the story and call the TV investigation off, I would be responsible inter alia for the non-birth of any baby he might father and for his own death. I had arranged to meet him in a couple of weeks and planned that the presenter would be wherever the meeting was to ask him questions. By the time the TV crew was in place, O'Mahoney was suspicious and put off the meeting. With the TV cameras in my study, I phoned his mum and told her how concerned I was about Ralph and how I really wanted to have a chat with him. She, too, expressed how worried she was. "But I have no idea where he is," I said. She gave me the address.

The TV footage shows a door opening just a bit, the interviewer saying: "Mr. O'Mahoney, Mr. O'Mahoney, Ralph. This is *60 Minutes* on TVNZ. We'd like a word," at which point the door closes and the camera picks up his name on a school calling card. "We couldn't stay. I can't imagine what was going on inside that house," Genevieve told me later.

I never heard from Ralph O'Mahoney again. A former colleague visited him and then visited me. He was unforthcoming as to anything O'Mahoney might have said. He told me O'Mahoney had started a company arranging children's school holidays. I tried searching for its activities, but drew a blank.

The programme had quite an impact on the New Zealand public, with questions from MPs. Peter Barlow travelled to the UK and met the DES, setting up a thoroughly sensible reciprocal arrangement whereby information about teachers banned but not convicted would be shared. *60 Minutes* received a gold medal for the best investigative journalism at a New York festival. The UK police and social services took an interest in the assault and I discovered the name of the victim. The HMC wrote (letter, 29 March 1994) that it "would take a dim view of any school which openly flouted List 99". This school was not open in its flouting. Only the head and a few trusted teachers knew. So, in this case, no "dim view" would be taken. I was not to discover what, if any, view was taken.

Once again, the media had alerted the public to a dreadful situation and, when they knew about something, something was done. Abusers might not be able to go to New Zealand, but there are plenty of other countries in the world.

The boy's parents decided not to prosecute to spare their ten year old the ordeal of a court case. The wider implications were that the abuser was free to travel the world and do as he wished. Maybe they assumed that O'Mahoney would change his ways after such a close call. Maybe they wanted to blot the incident from their collective minds. These incidents remain, however, and leopards don't change their spots. In protecting one child from an event, other children may be consigned to experiencing worse.

In 2014, Jed Nilssen agreed to take part in a documentary on Crookham Court School. The interview with him was in my home.

By this time, Jed was a man approaching fifty, a successful company director who for years had handled my telephone system. "It's funny," he told me (conversation, 28 April 2014), "I've been hoping all day that this filming would be called off. I felt really nervous." He retold the story, the events of more than thirty-five years before fixed in his mind. When he had spoken to me originally, he had simplified certain parts of it. Now he knew me, he felt able to talk freely. The memories were vivid—and raw. His voice trembled.

"I was quite a lonely child," he said. "I don't think I had many friends and in the evenings and weekends, there wasn't much to do. I was invited to Mr. Howe's room quite often and always with a group of boys and we would have hot drinks and biscuits and chat about this and that. It was a taste of home, I suppose, and this is what I missed at boarding school as my parents were away overseas and I just had my guardians. Some of the other boys would taunt me for being up there so often, but I didn't care. Ralph O'Mahoney was a young teacher, like a breath of fresh air, I suppose, and when he asked if I'd like to go to Newbury with him, I jumped at the chance. As we drove out, he asked if I'd rather go to a pub as it was a nice day and I agreed, of course. He bought me a shandy. I'm not sure I'd had alcohol before. He had one, too. He sat alongside me on one of those wooden pub benches in the garden. I remember he sat very close so that his leg was touching mine. He may have put his hand on my leg, I can't remember, but in any case, he was in what I saw as my personal space and it made me feel uneasy. He put his face close to mine and he said, "What things do you do with Mr. Howe?" I told him that we chatted and had hot drinks. "No," he said. "I mean what things do you do with Mr. Howe in his bedroom?" I told him I didn't "do things", but he wouldn't let go of the idea. "What do you and Mr. Howe do when you go into his bedroom?" I knew he was asking about sexual things. I just kept telling him I did nothing. "Well, whatever you do with him, would you like to do these things with me?" I told him, "No, I wouldn't." We left the pub and he drove me back to the school. Not another word was spoken between us. A couple of days later, he was going up the stairs to his room and he saw me. "I want to speak to you. Come up to my room," he said. "No," I said. He talked to me on the stairs. "What I said to you about doing things, I think you got it wrong. I didn't mean what I said. Just forget it." I told him I would.

But Jed certainly had not forgotten anything. The events of that sunny Saturday afternoon in 1978 remain firmly etched in his memory: Ralph O'Mahoney, his lavender Hillman Imp, the pub, the shandy, the proposition.

"I wonder what would have happened if I had gone into his room. It might all have been different."

I thought of all the damaged people I had spoken to while writing this book.

"It might. You were being groomed. You had already become complicit by keeping his proposition a secret. It's so easily done."

"And I never told anyone, except you. My parents don't know even now. Who could I have told? No one would've believed me anyway." For a moment, he was a boy again, a schoolboy making up for a mistake. "But I'd go to court now if a case came up."

The following day, thirty six years after the event, he reported the incident to the police.

I had not realised the significance of Ralph O'Mahoney's having "loved every moment" at Crookham Court, or of his sorrow that he had told me about when one of the boys was unhappy, or of his feeling rejected to the point of tears when that same boy would not accept his help. All the signs were there and I missed them all. Even when the boy told me after he had left that, when he changed for cricket, O'Mahoney always stripped naked before getting into his whites. I just saw it as odd. It did not occur to me to see anything sinister in these excesses.

Another pupil remembered Ralph O'Mahoney. Out of the blue, he phoned me (April 2014). "It's preyed on my mind," the boy told me. "I knew something wrong was happening, but I didn't do anything. I feel really bad about this. Always will. When I was at Crookham in 1978, a boy came to me. He was the brother of my friend. 'Please cover for me,' he said. 'Say Mr O'Mahoney is taking both of us out for the day.' It was an exeat, a day when we were allowed out. The two of us were taken to Newbury in his car. I was dropped off there and O'Mahoney told me not to get back until the end of the exeat. O'Mahoney told me to say I'd been with them all day. He drove off with my friend. There's more. I remember O'Mahoney and the teacher, Adam Wilson, spent time together. Wilson and O'Mahoney said in front of me that this boy, my friend, went on holiday with them in a canal boat on the Norfolk Broads and was so drunk they had to undress him to get him to bed. 'Don't trust him,' Wilson said to O'Mahoney, looking at me. O'Mahoney said, 'He's harmless.' I knew something wrong was happening. I blame myself. I did nothing."

"And the car?" I asked the boy, now a man in his late forties.

"It was an odd one," he said. "A lavender Hillman Imp."

TWENTY-ONE

It was everywhere

Peter's remarks that his memories of the school at which he was assaulted were the best days of his life only highlight the hold a school exerts over its former pupils. For the boys of Crookham Court, an old boys association, other than the huggermugger group that met to laud its work between 1961 and 1966, simply did not exist. Many were reluctant to admit their connection with the place and, much as they may have liked to maintain contact with their boyhood friends, in the absence of any office or institution, they drifted apart. With the advent of Facebook, those who knew of the existence of the Crookham Court page were able to put up photos and memories and to be told that various people would be at "The Travellers Friend" on a certain Saturday in June each year.

"Shouldn't it have an apostrophe?" my ten-year-old son, Piers, asked as soon as he arrived. None of my former pupils to whom I had tried to teach English had noticed. Over the years, different old boys came to these gatherings, just a handful at a time. The conversations were wide-ranging. Generally they were about matches played thirty years before; lately about the problems they were having with their children.

(Conversations, Crookham Court reunion, 7 June 2014): "He smokes too much marijuana," one lamented. "So what's the right amount?" did not generate a discussion about parenting. I drifted to a boy I had last seen forty years before.

"Saw you on TV," he said. "About your children." He paused. "And your books." He paused again. "What are you writing now?" Not once during all the reunions had the subject of abuse been raised. That elephant had remained in the corner, winking slyly sometimes, but now it trumpeted and I couldn't resist the temptation.

"Oh right," was the answer. "I've often wondered what happened to that French teacher, Greville. He was having it off with my dorm prefect. Every night. There we were lying in bed and there was Alex stripping stark naked in front of us, absolutely stark naked. Everything came off. And then he'd put on his dressing gown. It was dark blue and he left it open so we could see there was nothing underneath. Then he'd wrap it round himself, do the belt up and walk out with a smirk on his face. 'Where are you going then?' we'd all say. He'd smirk again. 'Off to see your friend?' we'd all say and he'd be off. We all knew he was going to see Greville. I never saw him come back. I'd be asleep by then. We all knew what was going on. And then later, when we were both in a canoe, he made a grab for my balls. Yes, he was sitting facing me, my legs were wide apart and his hand went up my shorts. 'Get off', I told him. Never happened again. He was a bender."

Alex. A boy I had met several times in the years after he left; a polite boy, well-spoken and attentive and with absolutely no self-confidence; a boy with whom I had talked about Greville and to whose father I had spoken about him as he had sometimes given him lifts back to the Isle of Wight at the end of term. "… and we'd never have let him into the car if we'd had any idea what he'd been up to, would we, Alex?" And Alex had shaken his head. And Alex had said never a word; never a word about Greville and hardly a word about anything else.

"I couldn't take more responsibility," had always been his answer when it became clear he was in the same job at thirty-five as he had been at eighteen. "No, it's not for me," had been his reaction when his best friend offered him a job in a company he created, leaving him, at fifty, in the position he had always been in. Alex moved away and contact was lost. I had wondered about this boy and why he had no self-esteem; why he always undervalued himself. There in the pub, in this moment of clarity given to me casually forty years after the events, I realised that he had made his solitary journey to this man's room from the ages of fourteen to seventeen to achieve an attention that would leave him wracked with unspoken guilt for the rest of his life.

I drafted a letter to him saying inter alia:

> Other former teachers should be called to account for their actions. The only way to stop them is for them to be jailed.
>
> The thing is that their victims sometimes feel as complicit as the criminals, so clever have their abusers been in making them feel this way. But they are not and never were. They are victims of crime, however much they may have felt they were acting out of free-will.
>
> Greville is one of the criminals who has been mentioned to me many times. I am aware of his crimes against several boys. I now know what happened. I can give details of named officers at Thames Valley Police who would make the process of disclosure as confidential as they could.
>
> I do hope you will take this forward. It may have been forty years ago, but what happened was criminal behaviour and needs to be addressed.

I sent it to the friend who had offered him a job for his take on the contents and for an address. "He'd hang himself," was the immediate response. "He wouldn't be able to take the shame of anyone knowing. Anyway, his wife would probably open the letter." His friend was right. "She's not the girl we'd have chosen for him and we'd have loved grandchildren," had been the parents' reaction to his rather unexpected wife who, one can only assume, had become used to a husband on a low light and who would, I was sure, react with horror, as would his parents who had always been easily offended. No wonder he had said never a word; had kept the secret that continued to eat him up; had let an abuser go free. Logically, he would be reassured by the non-judgmental tone of my letter, be relieved to disclose, tell the police, and make a complaint. There would be an arrest, an investigation that would involve several boys from Crookham Court School in the '70s, a trial, a conviction, and an abuser removed from society. Logic has never been a part of this sort of crime, though.

In reality, absolutely nothing would happen. And nothing did.

The complicity with the criminal is so strong that, until they are ready to do so, the victims give nothing away. I have asked parents of victims if there was anything they could have spotted and only in retrospect are they able to look at small areas of behaviour that might have given them a clue, if they had an idea what they were looking for. It is from the abuser himself—and occasionally herself—that the clues need to be deduced. There are common features. Like the celebrities, Rolf Harris, Jimmy Savile, and Max Clifford, all of them have the chutzpah and confidence to appear to be doing what they always do, being who they always are. For some this is standing in front of the camera or on stage; for others, it's being in their room surrounded by books, music, or whatever their passion might be. It is their performance, their show. They are in control and are so practised in what they do most often and best that they know they are giving nothing away. But they are.

If the abused is with the abuser, it can be the proximity of the abuser to the victim that is the giveaway. It is part of the control exercised by the abuser that the victim's freedom is eroded. There is an inequality between the abuser and the abused, sometimes by age or status, and there would naturally be a physical distance that propriety would impose. The abuser is in the victim's personal space and the impression given by the abuser is that this is because of an easy-goingness that is part of the persona which is at odds with the demeanour of the victim whose personal space has been entered; an inappropriate physical closeness. This is how celebrities have scored. They are expected to be confident, extravagant in gesture, exuberant. Those they encounter will be far less so and will naturally keep a distance. Teachers can also be expected to be expansive. When Wilson was on the bed with Henry Scott it looked like two friends, not pupil and teacher, and should have set alarm bells ringing. That it did not was because it looked so open, so natural. The assumption was that this was so close that it must be as far it would get. "And oftentimes, to win us to our harm, the instruments of darkness tell us truths, win us with honest trifles, to betray's in deepest consequence" (Banquo in *Macbeth*, 1.3). Nothing appeared hidden, but everything of importance was. Wilson was hiding in plain sight.

The jocularity of the inappropriate topics of conversation in which Hoade engaged suggested a lack of seriousness, a throwing-away of the situation, when it was creating a bond of inappropriateness, a like-mindedness as to topic in the knowledge that the theoretical would be likely to turn practical.

"He used to give us wine and cigars," one of the boys told me about Cavendish-Coulson. He was already seeing how young boys reacted when he bent the rules. Already they were keeping a secret for him. He was testing just how far he could go. His cryptic message to me—"que je suis desolé(e)"—hinted to me enough about his sexuality so subtly that I could do nothing about it. That he had written it when he had been alone with a boy in his room should have alerted me, but I assumed that as he was so subtly open, there was nothing more.

At Crookham Court where, because the fees matched the services' grant, many of the boys were from forces backgrounds, not the wealthy families able to pay the huge fees that most private schools charge, it was easy for some teachers to adopt attitudes and mannerisms that spoke to the children of a lifestyle outside their experience, to impress them with an upper-class accent, to give them an attention that was absent from their everyday lives. These teachers adopted an air of entitlement. Several invented lofty family connections, large parental homes, and the fruity vowel sounds that hinted at public school backgrounds. They impressed their charges easily and could, in this small private school world, have what they wanted, who they wanted. There was no one to stand in their way. Confident and articulate people were choosing to be with youngsters with no social graces or refined culture. Always there was an incongruity, but an apparent openness that closed off any further questions. It was cleverly done.

Abusers are resourceful people. In early 2013, I contacted one who had been convicted to find out what it was like to be an abuser. My letter went to his old address. He was still there and, surprisingly, he responded. I agreed that our correspondence would be off-the-record, but one cannot unknow what one learns and I learned a great deal through our correspondence and eventual meeting at my home in May that year. It was strange to have him sitting in the same room and on the same sofa as so many victims. I could have written about him, but I suggested he should write about himself in a chapter that, I assured him, would carry no authorial comment apart from a heading and an ending which he would be shown. In return I also agreed that his name would not appear elsewhere. All the other words in the chapter that follows are written by "Douglas".

TWENTY-TWO

Douglas's story

This chapter is the testimony of Douglas, who taught at Crookham Court between 1985 and 1987, and in 1990 was jailed for six years for sexual offences relating to teenage boys at Crookham and at another school where he had previously taught.

In April 2013 Ian Mucklejohn, who had been my colleague in the English department at Crookham Court during my two years at the school, contacted me to tell me that he was writing a book about the school. He suggested that I drive over to his house in Newbury to have a general conversation about the past and to discuss in what terms I might appear in the pages of his book.

Following this visit—and a number of subsequent email exchanges—I agreed to write a chapter telling my story in my own words, in order to give Ian the direct insight he wanted into how "someone like me" thinks and feels. In return Ian agreed that I be referred to as Douglas, rather than by my real name.

The point of this chapter is to explain, not to excuse. Of course I cannot justify what happened. It is always wrong for a schoolmaster to become sexually involved with his pupils. It does not matter whether the boy is willing, and it does not matter if the age difference between the two is small, as applied in the case of the first relationship I had after I started teaching, when I was in my early twenties and the boy in his late teens. (By the time of the Crookham offences the age difference was considerably greater.)

The reason it is always wrong is that it disrupts the "contract" between teacher and pupil, and indeed between teacher and parent—for parents send their children into the care of those that they believe to be responsible professionals, not seducers. In addition, an improper relationship of this kind is wrong because it complicates the young person's life; and, if the teacher and the pupil are both male, it may lead to a boy questioning his own sexual nature at a time when it is not yet fully formed. Sexual exploration and experimentation in adolescence should be with boys or girls of the young person's own age, not with adults.

I should make an important point at the start. Since the day I left Crookham over a quarter of a century ago, I have not committed a sexual offence of any kind—and I would not be so foolish as to make this statement if it were untrue, since it would doubtless provoke someone to come forward to contradict it.

Many offenders, not least sex offenders, revert to their old ways when they leave prison. So how was it that I did not? I did not receive treatment in prison, since in my day treatment programmes for sex offenders were a fairly new concept, and there were none in place at any of the prisons where I served my sentence.

One important factor in my not reoffending was that after I left prison in 1993 there was never again a context in which I could meet teenage boys. Another was that—partly perhaps as a result of the life-changing experiences I had gone through—the heterosexual part of my personality that had lain latent gradually surfaced, and I began to have relationships with women.

Readers of this book will, of course, judge me harshly in all kinds of ways—but would, I imagine, judge me all the more harshly if I attempted to self-exculpate. Also, if this account is to have any point, it is important that I say what I genuinely believe, rather than what I think readers would wish to hear.

Anyone who has spent any significant period of time in prison—I served three years of a six-year sentence—will know that there are many men in prison who shed crocodile tears; or who suddenly "find God" while they are inside, only (almost certainly) to lose him again once they are free; or who self-lacerate in an attempt to secure early parole. In the case of sex offenders such demonstrations are rarely sincere, because of the complex psychology behind offences of this nature.

There are doubtless some sex offenders who revel in depravity for the sake of depravity, or who enjoy having physical and sexual power over human beings weaker than themselves. Most, however, are otherwise decent men who lack the self-discipline or the moral sense to resist or control powerful impulses. An outsider standing on one of the wings at, for example, HMP Usk—a prison given over entirely to sex offenders, where I spent almost a year of my sentence—would see a cross-section of entirely normal-looking members of society: clergymen, accountants, journalists, plumbers, and plasterers, men no different-looking from their counterparts "on the out", as prisoners say. I remember a senior prison officer at Usk once pointing to a fellow-inmate—a seemingly amiable individual, who was serving a long sentence for molesting very young girls—and saying, "There are some very nice people in here who have done terrible things."

Human beings are adept at justifying the bad things they do, and one reason that it is difficult to prevent reoffending among sex offenders is that most do not believe they have done anything wrong. A thief or a fraudster will usually be happy to accept that he has committed a crime, although he may justify it to himself in terms such as, "It was a large firm, so what does it matter?" or, "He's much richer than me, so he can easily afford it." However, most sex offenders genuinely believe that the relationship with the boy or girl with whom they were involved was as real and valid as a normal adult relationship. In my own case, during the dozen years or so when I was sexually involved with teenage boys, it truly never for a moment crossed my mind that what I was doing was wrong, or that it might be damaging—although I was of course aware that it was not something a schoolmaster should be doing, and that therefore I was "breaking the school rules". To a non-offender, this may seem implausible, but for most sex offenders deviant behaviour is their "normal".

In addition, the question of the context of the times is relevant. The period of my offending was between 1975 and 1987. When I was growing up—I turned ten in 1961—attitudes to men having sex with teenage boys were very different from those of today. Terms such as "child abuser" and "paedophile" were not in use. In those days men who interfered with prepubescent children were known as child molesters, and were despised. Men who had sexual relations with teenage boys were referred to as pederasts, and did not attract the odium they attract today. If these matters came to light, such men went to prison—the sentences were relatively light in those days—and the world moved on. Occasionally a high-profile case made headlines, but for the most part these were matters that barely appeared on most people's radar.

Equally, for those emotionally and sexually attracted to teenage boys—the correct term is "ephebophile"—there was (and is) no shortage of reinforcing material in mainstream culture. I will give two examples.

One of the books on the reading list I was sent before I went to university in 1969 to study English was Christopher Isherwood's collection of linked short stories, *Goodbye to Berlin*. One story, "On Ruegen Island", dealt with a relationship between a man and a teenage boy, and reading this story made a profound impact on me. There was a shock of recognition and reinforcement. Here was a famous author writing about a sexual relationship between an adult and a teenage boy as though it were entirely normal and acceptable.

Then, in 1971, while I was still at university, Visconti's film of Thomas Mann's novella *Death in Venice* was released. Although in this case the main character's obsessive love for a teenage boy never had a physical expression, the film conveyed no hint of moral disapproval. This film, too, had a great effect on me, reinforcing as it did the "normality" of my own emotions and desires.

It is also important to point out that for many sex offenders—and this was certainly the case for me in those days—their deviant desires are so embedded that they in effect have no other option apart from celibacy. Ian has asked me at what age I realised I was attracted to boys. The answer is, from well before the age of puberty. When I was eight or nine I was already having strong "crushes" on other boys at school. For many people this kind of thing is a passing phase, but this was not so for me. Throughout my adolescence and until my late thirties my emotional and sexual focus remained entirely on boys in their teens. During my four years at university I had no contact with boys, so such very little sexual activity as I engaged in consisted of a few unsatisfactory and incomplete encounters with fellow-undergraduates of either sex.

I did not go into teaching in order to seduce boys—sexually inexperienced as I was, I had no idea that this would happen—but I did go into teaching because I wanted to be among boys. A psychiatrist who assessed me at the time my case was being prepared concluded that the roots of my offending were emotional rather than sexual. The emotional imperative is just as strong as the sexual—although of course the one often leads to the other.

Soon after I left university, I started teaching at a moderately well known public school I will call Northborough College, and within not much more than a year I embarked on a relationship that lasted for three years. I was twenty-three when it started, and the boy was seventeen. Over the ten years I taught at the school I had a number of relationships with boys. Sex is a very powerful instinct, and in his teenage years a male is at his sexual peak and often open to experimentation. Most of the boys with whom I was involved at Northborough were outgoing, confident, good at games; many were already sexually experienced with girls.

I remember a prison officer at HMP Reading, where I spent the first three months of my sentence, asking how these things came about. He was genuinely puzzled. But the answer is that they come about in much the same way as normal relationships. You are attracted to someone. You befriend them. You sense how the land lies and, if everything seems promising, you proceed. Usually, needless to say, I made the running, but this was not invariably the case. On a couple of occasions while I was at Northborough a boy who had guessed where things stood made it clear from his body language when he visited me in my study that he was interested in something happening.

As is the case with all sex offenders, there is the initial moment when the Rubicon is crossed; and of course that crossing of the river should never take place. When I visited Ian in May 2013, I told him about a particular master at Northborough College whose emotional focus, like mine, was indubitably on teenage boys; and indeed for a couple of years during my time at the school there was one very good-looking boy who was a constant visitor to his study. However, I am certain that nothing untoward ever happened. Such restraint—a firm drawing of the line—is not only appropriate but also admirable. Whatever his fantasies and desires may have been, he resisted them.

When I left Northborough it was not because a relationship with a boy had come to light. I was dismissed from the school because of an approach I made to a boy to whom I was attracted and had put out feelers. He discussed this with a couple of his friends, and then came to my study one day with a dictaphone (a small tape recorder) hidden in his clothing, and encouraged me to develop the theme of my interest in him. The recording was then taken to his housemaster, who went to the headmaster; and within a few hours I had left the school.

It was the early Eighties. Things were very different thirty years ago. I had taught at Northborough for ten years and, as far as the headmaster knew, this was the first time I had misbehaved. In those days it would have been common to give a second chance to a master who had, as it would then have been seen, slipped up in quite a small way. This was before most ordinary people knew of the obsessive nature of many men with a sexual interest in teenagers (or children, as the case might be). The headmaster of Northborough was perhaps naïve, but I had given the school excellent service for a decade. He had an otherwise good view of my character, and he believed there would be no recurrence. Nonetheless, while he agreed to write me references for future teaching jobs, he made it clear to me that these would include a full account of the circumstances that had led to my dismissal, albeit moderated by his belief that it was an isolated incident that would not be repeated.

Needless to say, with this caveat included, I found it almost impossible to get another teaching post—but Crookham Court was willing to take me, and I started teaching there in September 1985. As far as I can remember, my past was not discussed at my interview. Subsequent events have of course revealed that the school's proprietor, Philip Cadman, was himself a pederast, but I do not believe that this was the reason he employed me. Nonetheless, in view of his own sexual nature, it is safe to say he would not have been outraged by what he had learned from the headmaster of Northborough about the reason for my dismissal.

I did not return to teaching in an independent boys' secondary school with the cynical intention to go back to my old ways. I did so because I loved teaching and I loved being among boys. Indeed for the first year or so I resolutely resisted all temptation. There was one boy with whom matters came very close, but I held back. In the end, however, the old imperatives proved too strong, and there were two boys with whom I became sexually involved, Barry and Dan. It is likely that both of them will read this book, and it is right and indeed important that I should take this opportunity to apologise to them.

The consequences of my intervention in Barry's life when he was in his early teens appear to have been very unhelpful. I am aware of this because in May 2013 Ian Mucklejohn told me something of Barry's current circumstances. I know nothing of Dan's subsequent life, and I hope the same does not apply to him. It may do.

The fact that the sexual activity was, in both cases, in the context of a genuine friendship is neither here nor there. Indeed, paradoxically, this may have made it more difficult for them both to untangle themselves from the past. I have read that, if a boy afterwards has no doubt in his mind that the man with whom he was involved was in every way a monster, that fact may make it easier to move on; but if the man was someone whose friendship he valued, it can be more difficult.

During my conversation with Ian he said that one of the issues he wanted to examine in his book was the extent to which damage can arise as the result of the eruptions that often follow when these matters come to light. This is a controversial subject, but I will nonetheless address it.

The first thing to make clear is that the person who stands at the beginning of any chain of events must take responsibility for all the consequences that follow, regardless of whether he foresaw or anticipated them. This was a subject that was discussed on one occasion in the library at HMP Leyhill, the last of my three prisons, where two of my fellow prisoner-librarians were men of a similar background to myself who had committed similar offences, although neither of them had been teachers.

One of the men—I will call him Charles—accepted, as I did, that we had to take responsibility for any subsequent events. The other man, Gerald, did not. He took the view that society's stance on sexual relationships between men and boys was misguided, and that therefore it was not his fault if adverse consequences arose from what he believed to be society's wrong-headedness. A few years later I read in a newspaper that he was back in prison, serving an even longer sentence. He had returned to his old ways, and this was the third time he had come before the courts for having sex with boys.

After I left Crookham, I kept in touch with one or two members of staff and a couple of the boys. All the news I had of Barry during the eighteen months or so between my being dismissed and the school closing indicated that he appeared to have settled back comfortably into school routine. Indeed I was told that, a few weeks after I left, he went into the school office and asked if he could have my address because he wanted to write to me to find out how I was "going on". Needless to say he was not given it.

When I saw Ian in May 2013, and he told me what he knew of Barry's present life, I was moved to suggest that it might help him to come to terms with the past if Barry and I were to meet, in some carefully considered context and with another person present. But Ian did not think this would be a good idea.

I used to take Dan out in my car, which he enjoyed driving in fields of stubble. Once we went to the town where he had grown up. My advances to him were always tentative and, since he was clearly ambivalent about them, in general I did not persist. There was, however, one sexual episode, when he and another Crookham boy came to stay with me at my house in Wales during the summer of 1987.

With the benefit of hindsight, I think that Dan may have been a troubled soul in those days. What he needed was my friendship and support, and, although he did receive these, it would have been better if our friendship had not been complicated by my sexual interest in him.

Barry too came to stay with me in Wales, on two occasions. We explored the countryside and took long drives across mid-Wales. I never had any indication that Barry was uneasy about the sexual side of our relationship, but there may have been an underlying unease—reflected indeed in the episode that led to my dismissal from Crookham.

That evening, Barry came to my sitting room between supper and prep to ring his parents, as he often did—there was generally a queue for the boys' payphone in the main corridor. We did not engage in any sexual activity. Barry's call home continued a few minutes after the bell had rung for the start of prep, and after he left my room I heard him having an altercation in the lobby area below with a prefect who was remonstrating with him for being late.

This altercation for some reason developed into a conversation with a wider remit, which ended with Barry telling the prefect about his relationship with me. The prefect took Barry to see Alex Standish, who took him to Michael Gold, the headmaster; and I was at once removed from the school. I was not, however, reported to the authorities or to the police. In 1987 that would not have been unusual. Today it would be all but inconceivable.

If this chapter is to serve any purpose, it must, as I indicated at the start, be rigorously honest, so—at the risk of attracting hostility in some quarters—I need to say that I do not believe that relationships between men and teenage boys are always wrong. It depends, among other things, on the context (it must not be in a school); the relative ages of the two; and the personality of the boy.

After my dismissal from Crookham, it appeared most unlikely that I would ever be able to return to teaching. However, special circumstances applied in the case of the school where, a year or so later, I was able to obtain another teaching job. The school in question, which I will call Madeira House, was the small preparatory school, by then co-educational, that I had attended as a pupil thirty years earlier. Indeed it was there that, as I mentioned earlier in this chapter, I had had my first crushes on other boys, when I myself was a boy.

The headmaster from my time as a pupil was now the principal, and another master from my time was the headmaster. A third master from thirty years before still taught at the school part-time. I was therefore someone they knew, and they were relaxed about references. As far as I remember, I used old testimonials, and no one was freshly contacted about me.

Returning to the school that I had myself attended long before felt like a kind of redemption. I knew that there was no danger of my reoffending, since the boys were all younger than any I had ever been involved with. In any case I was not a resident master. I lived ten miles away.

But my past was waiting to catch up with me. In the spring of 1989 I learnt from my contacts at Crookham that the school was beginning to fall apart, as the result of a power struggle between Michael Gold and Philip Cadman.

Gold had found it impossible to work with Cadman, as indeed had his predecessor. At some point Gold and Alex Standish—who to all intents and purposes served as deputy headmaster—happened upon evidence that suggested that Cadman had had a sexual relationship with Barry's elder brother, Peter, when Peter had been at Crookham. Gold and Standish hoped to use this fact to allow them to wrest control of the school from Cadman.

They contacted Peter and Barry's parents; drove to their house; and confronted them with their suspicions. Although the parents had, understandably, been furious and upset eighteen months earlier after they had learnt of my relationship with Barry, they had taken a pragmatic approach at that time; and Barry had remained at Crookham, where he was happy. But now they were incandescent to discover that their elder son too had been seduced by a master at the school.

Crookham crumbled and closed; and I was back in the frame. I was arrested and my house was searched. Among my papers was found evidence that led to the Northborough past being revealed. Had the court been aware only of my relationships with Barry and Dan, I would have received a lesser sentence; but the offences at Northborough were also taken into consideration, and I was given six years in prison.

Ian has asked me to comment on the culture at Crookham Court. Was there, he says, something corrupt about the entire establishment?

I was at Crookham for only just over two years of its troubled history, and obviously I cannot comment on what the school was like before or after my time. All I can do is give a sense of the school as I knew it.

Crookham was eccentric, certainly, but I cannot say that I think that its culture was corrupt. The vast majority of the boys passed through the school without being subjected to sexual advances from masters, and I never heard of any homosexual activity among the boys themselves.

Crookham must have undergone as much scrutiny as almost any school in history. My guess, however, is that, if any boys' boarding school of that era had been similarly turned inside out, sex offenders would have been discovered. There have in recent years been historical scandals involving a number of schools, not least St. Paul's, one of Britain's most famous public schools. As in the case of Crookham, once the tip of an iceberg is sighted, what lies beneath often turns out to be substantial.

Hard though this is to believe today, in the Seventies and Eighties few eyebrows were raised if unmarried masters at independent boarding schools chose to spend much of their free time entertaining pupils. Indeed it was generally felt to be a good thing. In my own case, most of the entertaining I did at both Northborough and Crookham involved groups of boys—and, at Northborough, often girls as well, for the sixth form was co-educational—and this entertaining was in general entirely proper and above board. At both schools it was rare for me to be alone with just one boy; but opportunities were found. Today, procedures are doubtless in place at most boarding schools to ensure that it is difficult for a boy and a master to be alone together, and I would imagine that "salons" such as mine are looked at with some attention. This, together with greater awareness and changed attitudes, probably means that relationships between masters and boys are now rare.

In my time Crookham was not an unhappy school, but, as I have said, I cannot speak for other eras. The headmaster for most of the period I was there was an efficient administrator, and indeed when he left it was because he had decided he simply could not work with Philip Cadman, who constantly undermined his attempts to run a tight ship. Cadman was a kind of Lord of Misrule. He seemed to prefer chaos to order, and to enjoy boys taking advantage of him.

Ian has told me that one of the themes he is addressing in this book is what lessons can be learnt from the Crookham story. As elsewhere in this chapter, I can only answer for myself and from my own experience.

As already indicated, I believe that procedures and practices in boarding schools have been considerably tightened up over the years, partly indeed following the furore over Crookham. Beyond that, I suppose, it is a matter of constant alertness and constant vigilance, with the necessity that the default approach should always be one of suspicion rather than trust. That is a regrettable situation, and one that I am afraid that I and thousands like me, whether in schools or elsewhere, have helped to bring about—for it is a sad state of affairs where suspicion

> has to inform all interaction between adults and young people, and where, as a result, it is difficult for entirely benign inter-generational friendships to flourish.

* * *

The above are the words of a convicted sex offender. He was a colleague. It is unusual for an offender of this type either to acknowledge his guilt or to be willing to write about his crimes. In return for his contribution, I agreed to anonymise Douglas. It was not a difficult decision to make. It is Douglas's mindset rather than his real name which is of interest.

Douglas describes Crookham Court as being eccentric, but not corrupt. These are subjective terms. The efficient headmaster he refers to lived with and had a civil partnership with his long-term boyfriend for twenty-five years after the school closed. They had started when the boyfriend had been a pupil at Crookham Court School.

TWENTY-THREE

Douglas's victims' stories

So prolific an offender was Douglas that it is maybe unsurprising that, after he had presented me with his piece, two of his victims made contact with me.

Richard (not his real name) is one of the boys at Northborough who was abused by Douglas. He sees right through the words to the deeds and lives every day with the consequences of what was done to him as a child.

This is what Richard has to say:

> "Douglas" and the damage he did to me thirty-five years ago still make it so hard for me to see myself as a victim, although everyone tells me this is what I am. I did not experience the befriending that Douglas mentions, nor did I ever have a relationship with the man. He was a master manipulator. He manipulated everyone and every situation was contrived. He is driven by his ego, a psychopath for want of a better description. There were horrendous consequences to my life as a result of Douglas coming into it. My overwhelming feeling now is one of self-loathing.
>
> I was an awkward boy and found making friends difficult when I was a teenager. I made a perfect target

for Douglas and the other abusers who were employed at the school. Douglas was not the only one: there were as many as six individuals operating within the school. I was isolated, comparatively friendless. Douglas knew this, having made a point of taking his time and doing his research methodically before selecting each victim. That he was my tutor made contact easy, routine even, gave him access to my personal details, my weaknesses especially and even an entrée into my family and my parents' trust. He knew that I was homesick. I was not a sexually mature young man when, five weeks after joining the school, he started to groom me. Like all the victims, I was just thirteen. I was a child. Most of those he abused were pretty boys. The sporty, experienced-with-girls types are not part of my recollection.

A gentle touch on the knee progressed to the point a couple of months later from which there was no returning. It just went on and on. I simply stripped out of habit. He tried buggery once, but I wouldn't have that. The sex continued sometimes two or three times a day. His bedsit was at the top of the building at the end of a wooden corridor, along which he could hear people arriving, allowing him time to move away from his victims, reducing the likelihood of his being caught in the act. The man was insatiable. It's a wonder he had time to mark the prep. He was at it all the time. I felt a sense of control in that I could tell on him at any time and he knew that. That gave me power over him, or so I thought. Not once did I use this power, however, and he knew that he was safe with those whom he had taken beyond the point of no return. No boy whom he had brought beyond that point would ever tell. When his end came, it was a boy he had never touched who decided to record him and expose him for what he was.

In the fullness of time other teachers were sacked from Northborough and some were arrested. Another abusive teacher had me as his victim. My behaviour deteriorated and I underachieved academically. It was thirty-five years before I was diagnosed with depression and post-traumatic stress disorder.

Eventually, I took action against Northborough School and obtained compensation. During legal/police inquiries back in the 1980s, I was shown diaries that Douglas kept, describing hundreds of encounters with different boys, the prices he paid, and the "league table" he kept comparing us against each other. One thing that stuck out was his total contempt for the headmaster of Northborough School—how he had laughed internally as he had got away with it.

Douglas is like Jimmy Savile: an egotist, a liar, if they held a mirror to their souls they would be horrified at the reflection staring back at themselves. Savile used charity and TV as a cover, Douglas used teaching and entertainment for his cover. Douglas says he no longer offends, but I find that hard to believe, he so was demanding at Northborough.

I couldn't confront my abuser in court now. I can't face being torn apart by, who knows, a paedophile barrister in front of a paedophile judge. It's all covered-up. The police have managed to lose all the evidence. All that remains is the certificate of conviction.

I know that Douglas moved on to Crookham Court with a reference that Cadman found perfectly acceptable, but I find it unlikely that he moved from one school to another where abuse was rife as mere coincidence.

Richard did not find it easy to write about the crimes committed on him when he was a child.

> As no legal action had been taken against him, Douglas changed schools, abused some more boys and then, in the absence of a report on the crimes he committed at Crookham Court being given to any authority, went back to his old prep school for which no reference was needed. Had Peter not written to *That's Life!* who knows what Douglas might have done next. "I knew that there was no danger of my reoffending, since the boys were all younger than any I had ever been involved with," writes Douglas. I'm quite sure that age was not a barrier to him and he would take what he could get. There are plenty of teenage boys at prep schools.
>
> The "friendship" that is stressed in Douglas's piece, that became "complicated by relationship", played no part in his offending with me. There was no friendship; no relationship except that of a teacher and a victim. Like all abusers he has left behind a legacy of loathing and irreparable damage. His chapter is an example of his manipulation.

As for the reference to "returning to the school that I had myself attended long before felt like a kind of redemption. I knew that there was no danger of my reoffending, since the boys were all younger than any I had ever been involved with"—through the "Survivors" Facebook page I have been contacted by yet another of Douglas's victims who attended that very same prep school and at the age of eleven became only too aware of his reoffending.

Once again it is the voices of children decades later that are telling what abuse really is.

AFTERWORD

Teaching at Crookham Court brought me into contact with teachers who are child abusers, in these cases abusers of boys. The abuse I write about is the institutionalised sexual abuse of boys. At the time, I was unaware that that a significant number of my former colleagues were abusers and I started writing this book as a contemporaneous account of a bizarre school that bore the hallmarks of Evelyn Waugh's "Decline and Fall". It was in the late 1980s that I realised there was a far darker dimension to the events there and saw that it was about criminals and victims. Writing this book has enabled me to ask the few of the criminals I managed to make subsequent contact with questions about the origin and nature of their obsession. The answers to my questions were elicited with some difficulty.

"Crookham was not an unhappy school." In April 2015, I was asked to meet a former pupil. It was his "advocate" who requested the meeting. I could see why. The boy had been a normal 16 year-old when he started, but was now a man unable to make eye-contact; unable to converse except via his "advocate"; a man who had realised that the experiences he had accepted as the norm since childhood were so utterly abnormal that he needed help to cope with this knowledge; a man left unable to trust anyone. His personality had been subsumed into that of his teacher and rendered him incapable of independent action. He had become so taken-over at an early age that he was unable to act on his own initiative.

One of the abusers, I shall call him Edward (not his real name), objected to my referring to him as a "child abuser". Edward had been a colleague. He was a slight man in his mid-thirties with wavy brown hair, formal in his jacket and tie and with a touch of the young fogey about him. As a new colleague, I took him for dinner to The Bell in Ramsbury. We chatted about literature and philosophy and I sensed his pacifist leanings which struck me as in keeping with his vegetarianism. A gentle man, I thought, with a slight, self-deprecating hesitation in his voice and a modest demeanour. Not one to work with actively to put an end to Cadman, though. He was a resident master with a small bedsit at the top of a flight of stairs in what had been the servants' quarters of the house. I saw little of him. He was of the "man among children and child among men" type of teacher, apparently sincere, committed even, not particularly spontaneous in adult company, and with a string of children visiting his room to listen to music and to chat. And the children were, I observed, not the chatty, convivial ones. These were boys who maybe needed to be brought out of themselves. A generous man and a dedicated teacher who constructed his life around children. Or so I assumed.

I was, of course, proved wrong. "I never abused a child," was his retort. He had been affronted by my use of the term in relation to his many crimes. He told me that it is a term widely used, but it has as many meanings as the user or the hearer imposes on it, informing me that its sense is of men who interfere with children before the age of puberty and that it is a replacement for the term "child molester". He assured me that everyone refers to under-elevens as children and that primary school teachers use the term constantly. Teenage boys, he assured me, are always described as teenagers, boys, or (when they commit crimes) youths. At none of the schools this abuser taught in did any teacher ever refer to the pupils as "children".

He stated categorically that he had never had sexual relations with a boy who was other than a sexually mature teenager. And that he never would have.

Did he really imagine my response would be, "Oh, that's all right then"? He did, however, give me his definition of the term. He informed me that "child abuser" is not a technical term, but a colloquialism with many different applications that is often used loosely. He was also concerned that "child abuser" and its close cousin "paedophile" are instant hate words and that neither applied to him. He was careful to define "paedophile" and assure me that it had a precise meaning that was removed from his inclinations. And, although he opined that instant hate might be the proper response to his conduct, he preferred the term "sex offender", although this was not a term he liked much either. He described it as "ugly" and maintained that it pigeonholed him, or more accurately, he corrected himself, described only part of what he is. I suggested that parents might really not be interested in the other parts of him. Knowledge of his desire to have underage sex with their sons would be quite enough.

"I always called the children at Crookham 'children'," I told him. "My sons are nearly fourteen and I call them 'children'. I call all my students who go right up to the age of eighteen 'children', because that's what they are."

He accepted that it is entirely subjective as to whether a boy is "emotionally sexually mature" and accepted that that his victims had been "in all probability", not emotionally ready for such a relationship. He accepted that a homosexual relationship between a teacher and pupil added "complications" that would not apply if it were heterosexual.

He assured me that he had never had a relationship with a boy who was not past puberty—and therefore "biologically mature" and, indeed, capable of having sex with a woman and becoming a father. How the abuser knew about a boy's biological development without taking his clothes off was a point that remained unexplored. As was the exact nature of the crimes themselves. All I managed to elicit was that the crimes were at the "lower end of the homosexual spectrum". That he had the boy's erect penis in his mouth was not denied. The abuser declined to give specifics on the grounds of "delicacy". Every aspect of every encounter was couched in euphemism.

The abuser also considered it was not essential to reveal "the arithmetic"—the term he used for the number of children whose lives he touched. I discovered it was in the hundreds.

He defined his crime in his own terms, so downgrading it that in his head it became not a crime at all. According to his syllogism, sexual acts happened between a consenting and mature younger person and an avuncular older friend.

What is utterly terrifying about the child abusers I have encountered is their refusal to accept that a crime has happened. More, there is an insistence that the acts were not coercive—"I never coerced anyone"—and were simply between people who happened to be of different ages and the same sex and who were enjoying themselves. The language of the initial desire, the grooming, and the abuse itself is so sanitised, so intellectualised, so "academicised" as to be unrecognisable as the crime it is. That it is an adult in a privileged and authoritative position who instigates the activity is unmentioned. The chaos the victim is left to deal with, if considered at all, is an unfortunate consequence. The mutual benefit of the encounter is stressed. That awfulness of a crime initiated by a man and enacted on a child does not register as no child was involved.

And that person remains a danger.

This abuser felt quite safe. So complicit had he made his victims in his crimes, so complicit did they feel having had the erection and orgasm that marked the crossing of the border, he knew they dared not talk. The mutually beneficial bond was for the benefit of one person only and that was not the child.

The argument that there was no coercion cannot be maintained. There was coercion from the moment the first inappropriate touch or suggestion was made. There was the teacher, the person in a position of authority, of trust, making the request that something should happen. No matter how willing the child, those words should never have been uttered; that movement should never have been made; that boundary should never have been crossed. That is the coercion. As long as a teacher, or any abuser can feel or can say "there was no coercion", that teacher has not accepted his responsibility, his guilt, his commission of a crime.

Edward was the stuff of nightmares, unlikely ever to be forgotten by his many victims. His guilty plea at his trial may have spared his victims a cruel dissection in the witness box, but it was not inspired by any feelings of guilt, pity, or remorse. His literary interests were his downfall. In the one telephone call he was permitted after his arrest, his words to a contact were listened into by the police. Before the contact had the chance to destroy the diaries as instructed, they had seized them. They contained meticulous records of over 1000 assaults on children. Also recorded were the sums of money he had paid to each child. Each crime recorded to be enjoyed again at will.

I have been contacted by many abused people, all of whom have been abused in a different way and have their unique suffering to deal with. What each of them has in common is that the very core of their being has been touched. Whether it was one encounter or many over a prolonged period or even a proposition, the damage has gone to the soul. This is what those who have not been abused find so hard to understand. This is what they must take on trust. The victims feel they cannot move on. The corrosiveness of abuse is in a league of its own. I know how hard it has been for those who have been so terribly damaged to talk to me and I thank them for being brave enough to do so. Child sex abuse needs to be demystified and the light of publicity shone into the dark corners of complicity in which it thrives. The time may come when child sex abuse is seen by children as a crime like the rest with a criminal and a victim—a crime that needs to be reported.

In the same way that I did not see or even consider the danger in the situations I encountered, neither did the victims. They did not see their teacher as acting in any other way than in their interests. They interpreted predatory desire as concern, kindness, friendliness. Their interactions became part of their life. By the time the true nature of the predator's ambitions became clear, the victim was trapped.

That these perversions exist is the first understanding. That they can happen in any position of trust is the second. Absolute transparency is the only way to interact. A professional needs to live life as though being followed by a TV camera crew. Secrecy and private moments are for private life and have no place in professional encounters.

We as a nation became less innocent in 1989 after the Crookham Court scandal. Esther told me, "David Mellor came to see me at the end of it and asked me if there was anything he could add to 'The Children Act'. Social services' ability to enter schools was introduced. It certainly alerted people to the culture of abuse."

In 1989, Robert Smithwick had a letter published in *The Newbury Weekly News* (15 June) under the heading "Disgrace saddens school's founder":

> As founder in 1961, and principal of Crookham Court School for 16 years until it was bought from me in 1977 by Philip Cadman, I have naturally been saddened to see on TV and read in the press of all the troubles and, now, the fear that it may have to close.
>
> I have been approached by Old Boys and staff of the school who feel it should be pointed out to those

who do not know its history that the school was, for 16 years, a caring, happy and efficient school, which gave a sound social and academic education to a great many boys.

It naturally takes some years to build up the necessary facilities and to achieve the teaching standards together with the traditions for a boarding school to achieve a state of efficiency that will satisfy Her Majesty's Inspectors.

In 1964 the school was granted "Provisional Recognition" and finally in 1973, after a full and thorough inspection Crookham Court was "Recognised as Efficient". I passed on such a school to Philip Cadman.

That which takes years to build up can collapse very rapidly.

The staff and boys who were at the school from 1961 to 1977 deserve to be distanced from the Crookham Court School of the 80s.

Robert Smithwick

Sadly, of course, they cannot be. The evil was present from the start. And those who were placed there from 1977 to 1989 certainly did not deserve what happened to them.

Such is the history of Crookham Court School.

> History ... the junction of a dizzying range of alternatives any one of which could have had a different outcome.
>
> History ... a commentary on the various and continuing incapabilities of men.
>
> History ... is the utter randomness of things.
>
> History ... it's just one fuckin' thing after another. (Alan Bennett—*The History Boys*)

History is unforgiving of those who make mistakes. Oversights, errors of judgment, incorrect assumptions, slips, some in themselves seemingly innocent, but the mistakes were compounded by other mistakes. Each wrong judgment led to lives being damaged; criminals being allowed to wreck children's lives. All the mistakes, all the crimes, were the result of actions and inactions by grown-ups. All the revelations were the voices of the child victims, speaking out.

Several of these, now middle-aged men, have emerged stronger. They have been believed and have seen their abusers exposed as criminals. This can make all the difference and is why victims need historic abuse cases to be pursued. The swirling eddies of evil that washed over and around Crookham Court School have, decades later, revealed the fundamental indomitability of the human spirit and the refusal of those whose souls were touched in childhood to remain victims.

The crimes happened so easily, so almost accidentally. And they could all happen again.

"Just one fuckin' thing after another." The adjective is what, ultimately, it was all about. The rest, as they say, is history.